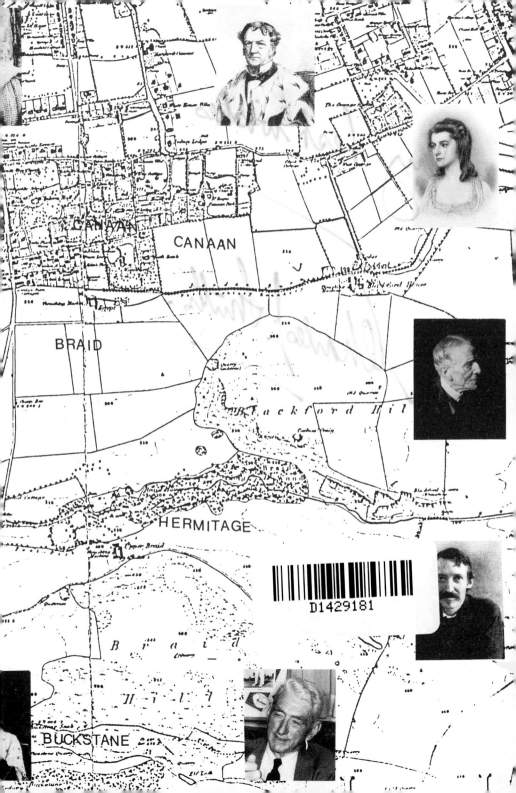

CANAAN

CANAAN

BRAID

Blackford Hill

HERMITAGE

D1429181

Braid

Hill

BUCKSTANE

Very best wishes

Charles J. Smith.

Historic South Edinburgh

VOLUME FOUR

Swanston Cottage,
a home of Robert Louis Stevenson
and his family

Historic
South Edinburgh

BY CHARLES J. SMITH

VOLUME FOUR

CHARLES SKILTON LTD

© Charles J. Smith 1988
Made and printed in Great Britain
and published by
CHARLES SKILTON LTD
Whittingehame House
Haddington, East Lothian

SBN 0284 98757 3

VOLUME IV

CONTENTS

FOREWORD AND
ACKNOWLEDGEMENTS

MUCH of what I wrote by way of a Foreword to Volume 3 applies equally to this further volume, but naturally certain additional points must be made. In the preparation of the material I have again found indispensable the ready assistance of so many people, either in their professional capacity when their help was much more than a formality, or as individuals, frequently the relatives of those about whom I have written. If my acknowledgement to them, (whose contributions naturally varied considerably), is necessarily brief, this is no measure of my gratitude.

Sources have again been those basic works referred to in my Introduction to Volume 3 or in the comprehensive Bibliography provided in Volume 2 of this work along with the additional biographical notes in this volume which give special information, in several instances derived from correspondence with people who, as close relations or friends, had a particular knowledge of the person concerned. However, in biographical research, libraries are the initial source of material, and in a book concerning Edinburgh people, reference to the indispensable and invaluable resources of the City Libraries Edinburgh Room is essential. I am most grateful, therefore, for the professional and patient assistance of Miss Sheena McDougall and her staff of this rich treasure house. Likewise, I am again deeply indebted to Mrs N. E. S. Armstrong, the City Libraries Head of Reference and Information

Services, who kindly and expertly tracked down information which otherwise I certainly would not have discovered. Mrs Armstrong also set out the bibliographical notes and undertook the rather Herculean task of compiling the index for both volumes, for all of which I am most grateful.

To Miss M. Burgess and the staff of the City Libraries Scottish Room and to Miss P. Minay and staff of the Fine Art Department, I am also much indebted. I also express my appreciation for much kind assistance from the staffs of the National Library of Scotland and Edinburgh University Library, to Mr Colin Will, of the British Geological Survey's Edinburgh departmental library section, who was most helpful, and to the Scottish Poetry Library. I have again enjoyed the kind assistance of Mrs Sheila Durham whose survey of those buried in Morningside Cemetery is a most valuable source of material.

Information concerning very many of the people presented in this volume just would not have been available without the kind co-operation of the following, to whom I am greatly indebted: Professor S. R. Checkland; Mr G. D. D. MacKinnon, WS., Aberdeen; Mr David Fraser and Mrs J. Warburton of the Royal Edinburgh Hospital; Mr Ian Gow of the Royal Commission on the Ancient and Historical Monuments of Scotland; Mr Wilfred Taylor; Professor J. S. D. Mellick, University of Queensland, Australia;

Mr Robert J. Naismith of Sir Frank Mears & Partners; Mrs Gulielma Dowrick (neé Lister), Wellington, New Zealand; Mr Tristram Clark; Mr R. Copland, formerly of Astley Ainslie Hospital; Rev. Father Allan White, O.P.; Rev. Father Brocard Sewell, Carmelite Order; Mrs Aileen Little; Mr Gilmour Main; Mrs H. Meikle; Mr W. H. Rutherford, secretary, the Royal Society of Edinburgh; Mr Sandy Harrison; Mr and Mrs R. A. C. Linzee Gordon of Cluny Castle; Dr Poppy Cooksey; Mrs Cecile M. C. Paterson, daughter of Professor Charles Barkla; Miss I. D. Wilkie; Mrs W. M. Little; Sir John Clerk of Penicuik; Mrs Margaret E. Fraser, daughter of Mr James S. Bennet; Major Alexander Trotter of Mortonhall; Miss Janet Ratcliffe Barnett; Mrs W. Cochrane; Professor Neil Campbell for very much help; Mr David Wallace, grandson of Dr Thomas Clouston, and his wife, Mrs Una Wallace, daughter of Dr David Strachan; Miss Lesley de Jean, former Lothian Health Board Archivist; Mr Norman Mair and Mr Ian Wood of The Scotsman sports desk; Mr F. H. Robarts, F.R.C.S.(E); the late Mr George Mutch; Mrs Deirdre Wedd, grand-daughter of Mr William Mair; Mrs Mary MacDonald; Mrs Genevieve Reid; Mrs Jane McGregor; Mrs Catriona Mac-Naughton; Mrs J. Perry, Head Teacher, and Miss Marie Clunie of South Morningside Primary School; Professor D. E. C. Mekie, Conservator, Royal College of Surgeons, Edinburgh Museum and Mr P. Edmond, C.B.E., F.R.C.S.; Mr Charles Allan, City Officer, City of Edinburgh District Council, Mr Brian McGuire, the Council's Assistant Director of Public Relations and Tourism and his colleague, Mr Rudi Ganrin; Dr Andrew Doig; Mr Malcolm Cant; Mr Brian Smith, Mr James Gray; Dr Allan Simpson; Mr Maurice Berrill; Dr Walter Stephen and Mr F. A. Ainslie.

For many of the portraits, I am again greatly indebted to the National Galleries of Scotland, Edinburgh and to various photographers as the captions indicate. Much kind assistance was again received from Miss Sheila Fletcher, Secretary to the Edinburgh University Pictures Committee. The professional services of Mr Bill Weir and his colleague, Mr Malcolm Liddle of the University Library Photographic Department have also been invaluable, especially their skilled ability to improve upon much rather unpromising material. My brother, Mr W. R. Smith has again rendered much greatly appreciated assistance. I am particularly indebted to Mrs Anne Craigie for typing what was at times a difficult manuscript. As in Volume 3, where a portrait could not be traced or obtained or was known not to exist, an illustration of special relevance to the person concerned has been substituted.

Grateful acknowledgement is made to the copyright holder of George Campbell Hay's poems and to the trustees of the W. L. Lorimer Memorial Trust Fund. I am pleased to record my sincere appreciation to Mr Charles Skilton for kindly publishing these further two volumes; to Mr Leonard Holdsworth, his colleague, for much encouragement and advice, and to the late Mr Eric L. Randall for patiently editing a lengthy and at times intricate manuscript.

Finally, as was explained in the introduction to my general historical volumes on South Edinburgh, as regards certain aspects of the biographies presented it is frequently impossible to be definitive. Nor are they the latest assessments or reassessments of the people concerned, which in many cases are continually being made by scholars. For many readers, these short biographies may simply provide an introduction to someone hitherto unknown to them and it is hoped serve as a stimulus to turn to lengthier and specialised works. Through the interest and diligent researches of other people, often originated or prompted by my work, new information is brought to light or people kindly write to me or telephone with additional data of which I was unaware when preparing my manuscript. Thus, the study of local history and the people of a district is an ongoing process and a work of collaboration. That the publication of these short biographies may possibly prompt readers to uncover new knowledge and some perhaps to publish it would be most gratifying.

CHARLES J. SMITH

1 · TIPPERLINN/
ROYAL EDINBURGH HOSPITAL

EBENEZER GAIRDNER

WHILE Morningside's beginnings in the early 1800s, or perhaps earlier, are a common source of interest to its residents today, in fact adjacent to it was another little village of much greater antiquity, appearing on record indeed as early as 1586 and perhaps existing even well before that date. Tipperlinn is of interest not only for its antiquity, but especially because here there lived and worked, perhaps for two centuries, a community of weavers who achieved some fame. And in the recent restoration of the north side of the West Port, the ancient lands of the "websters", as the weavers were known, with the replacement above one of the close entrances of this ancient craft-guild's emblem, dated 1735, and the words: "My days are swifter than a weaver's shuttle", one is reminded that the weavers of Tipperlinn had their links with their fellow craftsmen in the West Port.

While a number of the names of the old weavers of Tipperlinn remain on record, notably the family of Munnoch, nothing is known of them personally. However, of the "father" of the community, around 1770, a considerable amount is known, meriting for him a place amongst our "People" of South Edinburgh. This man was Ebenezer Gairdner, who, reputedly by a stroke of good fortune, earned for himself and his fellow craftsmen a "By Royal Appointment" warrant. In the 1770s

Insignia of the Weavers of Portsburgh, Edinburgh, 1735

Displayed in the restored West Port.
"My days are swifter than a Weaver's Shuttle".
From the Sculptured Stones of Edinburgh by John Geddie

the Tipperlinn weavers were already noted for their manufacture of damask tea-towels and table-cloths. One day, while Ebenezer Gairdner was delivering a supply of these to the owners of Leven Lodge, just on the northern fringe of Bruntsfield Links, he met the young Countess of Sutherland, an orphan, who was residing at Leven Lodge with her guardians. She was impressed by the Tipperlinn work and, it is said, when older and with some influence in royal circles, and when the weavers had produced a special table-cloth portraying "The Triumphs of Britannia", she obtained for Gairdner and his community a Royal Appointment to Queen Charlotte, plus an immediate order for 230 of the special table-cloths and the title "Damask Manufacturer to Her Majesty".

Many years ago, at an exhibition on the history of Morningside largely organised by the late Mr William Mair, author of a most valuable little book on the history of the district, one of the Tipperlinn table-cloths was on display, it is believed then the property of Miss C. Evans who resided in Morningside Park. All attempts by the present writer to trace this table-cloth and any other relics of the Tipperlinn weavers have sadly failed.

Gairdner's yarn-boiling premises were near the Vennel in the Portsburgh district at the foot of the West Port, an important and industrious websters' or weavers' quarter. Gairdner's son was Deacon of the Weavers Guild in 1798. Ebenezer Gairdner, perhaps encouraged and enjoying increased trade through his royal favour, opened a shop in the then new and fashionable South Bridge. He died in 1797 and was succeeded in the business by his son and William Munnoch. By the time of the establishment of the Western Department or West House of the asylum in Morningside, the Tipperlinn weaving industry seems to have been dying out, and eventually by about 1860 the asylum authorities had acquired, and soon afterwards demolished, the last of the craftsmen's two-storey cottages.

Two relics of the early Tipperlinn community remain. Built into the rear of the wall on the left at the entrance to the Royal Edinburgh Hospital's Young People's Unit (Tipperlinn House) is a Restoration Stone, dated 1660, which, as in many other parts of Scotland where the local people were Royalists, was probably placed in the Tipperlinn "High Street" to mark the restoration of the monarchy at that date. A short distance onwards down this roadway towards the main hospital, on the coping-stone of the low wall on the right, is an inscription cut into the stone, its letters just barely legible but of which "1796" can be deciphered. There would appear to be two sets of initials, and perhaps these are of husband and wife on what was once a marriage lintel on one of the old weavers' cottages. Expert treatment of this relic is required. The ancient village is, of course, commemorated by the nearby street name.

THOMAS GLADSTONES

IN the early records of Tipperlinn reference is made to what local boys apparently described with an air of mystery and perhaps suspicion as "the black works". Really, however, undue mystery there was none. This was a chemical plant and its "suspicious" product was oil of vitriol, or sulphuric acid. The enterprise had been founded in about 1770 at "Barrowmuirhead, not far from Leith" and the two partners were Steel, Gladstones & Co. The first named was Dr Thomas Steel, a doctor of medicine and a chemist, whose family for generations owned "Grangebank", the large rather uninviting house at Boroughmuirhead, which little district lay in the triangle formed by Morningside

Thomas Gladstones

From "The Gladstones" by S. R. Checkland
By courtesy of the author and Cambridge University Press

Road (originally Waverley Terrace and Marmion Terrace), Abbotsford Park and Colinton Road. The house still stands in the space reached by the little lane at the south side of the Baptist Church at Holy Corner. Dr Steel was later the principal partner in another chemical works which opened on the fringe of the Canaan estate, at what is now commemoratively named Steel's Place, where magnesia was manufactured for inclusion in Dr Gregory's mixture. No further details of Dr Thomas Steel could be traced, or any portrait.

The other partner in the Tipperlinn chemical works was Thomas Gladstones, grandfather of the celebrated Prime Minister, William Ewart Gladstone, who dropped the final "s" from his name. Thomas Gladstones

was born in Biggar in 1732. In the mid-18th century he came to Leith, where his elder brother the Reverend James Gladstones was Rector of Leith Academy. Thomas became a corn dealer and provision merchant. He married late in life Miss Nelly Neilson, daughter of an Edinburgh merchant, and his wife apparently was "the making of him" on account of her flair for commerce and trading. His own business prospered and he became lessee of Dalry Mills, near Leith, and built up a market in Greenland. The Tipperlinn sulphuric acid works were his next venture. One of the raw materials required for the chemical manufacturing process was brimstone (sulphur), obtainable from Italy, and Thomas Gladstones imported this, sending in return cargoes of herring from Leith to Leghorn. By 1840, contemporaneously with the expansion of the asylum and the steady disappearance of the village of Tipperlinn weaving community, the chemical factory may have constituted an obstacle to the hospital's further development. At any rate, it closed down soon after 1840 and was absorbed into Imperial Chemical Industries and its processes transferred to Glasgow. No further details of the "take-over" could be found in the archives of ICI.

ROBERT FERGUSSON AND DR ANDREW DUNCAN

TWO names are inseparable from any historical account of the Royal Edinburgh Hospital, originally described as "ane proper asylum for the insane", opened in 1813. Firstly, the famous Scottish poet Robert Fergusson, whose tragic and untimely death at the age of 24 occurred

Robert Fergusson

by Alexander Runciman
By courtesy of the National Galleries of Scotland, Edinburgh

in the City Bedlam in Bristo on October 16th 1774 from a form of melancholia. And, secondly, Dr Andrew Duncan, senior, who as a young visiting doctor had been appalled to witness the circumstances of the young poet's death and, on account of the lack of knowledge of the nature and cause of such mental disorders and their treatment at that time, was unable to give any assistance. He made it his resolve to spare no effort in having "ane proper asylum" established, which not until forty years later was he to see become a reality.

Robert Fergusson, born of humble parents in Cap and Feather Close off the High Street, was forced by his father's death to give up his studies at St Andrews' University, and accepted a rather boring post as a copy clerk in the Commissary Office

in Edinburgh. He did not allow this disappointment to vitiate his poetic genius and before long had his first work published, which was widely acclaimed for its depiction of the very essence of life in the Auld Reekie of his time. He has been compared with Robert Burns and by some critics preferred to him. Indeed Burns himself acknowledged his deep indebtedness to Fergusson when, having almost given up his own efforts, he was inspired anew. Burns it was who composed the epitaph on the gravestone which he himself caused to be erected over the young poet's long-neglected burial place in Canongate churchyard.

Dr Andrew Duncan's early efforts to obtain support, financially and otherwise, for "ane proper asylum" were of little avail. Only when he began to achieve considerable distinction in the medical world by succeeding Professor James Gregory in the Chair of the Institutes of Medicine and becoming President of the Royal College of Physicians, did he begin to evoke greater interest and the essential funding. The main source was £2,000 from the monies

Dr Andrew Duncan

by Henry Raeburn
Showing framed picture of new asylum building
By courtesy of the Royal College of Physicians, Edinburgh

and lands forfeited by the Highland chieftains who had supported the '45 Jacobite Rebellion, made available from Parliament by negotiation. Money also came from Scots in India and elsewhere. At last the foundation-stone of the new building was laid, on June 8th 1809, and the first patients admitted by July 1813. The original East House on the Morningside Estate stood between Morningside Road and Morningside Terrace, and Millar Crescent and the Jordan Burn, at the back of the north side of Maxwell Street, with a large gateway almost opposite Jordan Lane. Dr Andrew Duncan's perseverance stemmed not only from his conviction that the need for the new hospital was urgent but also from his boundless energy. He founded medical journals, opened the Royal Dispensary in Richmond Street, established the Caledonian Horticultural Society, and was still annually climbing Arthur's Seat on May 1st even in his early 80s.

Dr Andrew Duncan lived to see his hospital opened in 1813, was involved in its early management, and is commemorated by the modern Andrew Duncan Clinic, opened in 1965, nearly two centuries after Fergusson's death. The young poet whose tragic end had so powerfully motivated him used frequently in periods of depression to leave the city and seek peace in the country; he had known Morningside affectionately and nostalgically and was especially attracted by one part, of which he wrote:

THE HERMITAGE OF BRAID

Would you relish a rural retreat
  Or the pleasure the groves can inspire,
The city's allurements forget,
  To this spot of enchantment retire,

Where a valley and crystalline brook,
  Whose currents glide sweetly along,
Give nature a fanciful look,
  The beautiful woodlands among.

Oft let me contemplative dwell
  On a scene where such beauties appear;
I could live in a cot or a cell,
  And never think solitude near.

DR WILLIAM McKINNON

McKinnon House

Showing Pinel Memorial, foreground, centre
Photograph by Mr W. R. Smith
By courtesy of the Royal Edinburgh Hospital

FOR very many years, the two principal sections of what was originally "ane proper asylum for the insane", or Morningside Asylum, were named, simply on a geographical basis, the East House (the first premises to be opened in 1813, on the east side of what is now Morningside Terrace) and, 29 years later, the Western Department, or West House, designed by the noted architect William Burn and opened in 1842. The West House was entered from Morningside Terrace or from the west, through the old village of Tipperlinn. It was as a tribute to the distinguished, if extremely short period of service as the first Physician Superintendent in charge of West House, that some years ago it was named McKinnon House.

171

Dr McKinnon is yet another of the notable people once resident in or associated with South Edinburgh about whom unfortunately little remains on record. Through the kind assistance of Aberdeen City Libraries, the University Library, and Mr G. D. G. MacKinnon of an Aberdeen legal firm founded by an early member of the family, a brief outline of Dr William McKinnon's background and career can, for the first time, be compiled.

Dr William McKinnon's great-grandfather was a native of Arran, his grandfather a shipwright in Greenock, and his father founded the Aberdeen iron founders business W. McKinnon and Co., which is still in existence. His uncle, Lachlan, was a shipmaster in Aberdeen who commanded several vessels based there. Dr William McKinnon was born in Aberdeen in 1815. While his brother Lachlan served in their father's iron-foundry business, William pursued an academic career, gaining a Master of Arts degree at Aberdeen University in 1832, a Doctorate of Medicine at Edinburgh University in 1836, and later the Fellowship of the Royal College of Physicians of Edinburgh. In June 1837 he was successful against two other applicants for the post of House Surgeon and Apothecary at Aberdeen Lunatic Asylum and appointed for six months until December 3rd 1837 at a salary of 50 guineas per annum plus board. He was re-appointed a lecturer in comparative anatomy in the Medical School of Marischal College, a new post, on September 3rd 1839; but soon afterwards, in February of the next year, was taking up a post "in an Institution in Edinburgh".

The Institution in Edinburgh was the Royal Edinburgh Lunatic Asylum and Dr McKinnon's appointment as the first Resident Medical Superintendent was made to coincide with the opening of the newly completed Western Department which was one day to bear his name. Dr McKinnon's appointment also preceded a great influx of additional patients due to the asylum's decision to admit "pauper patients" from various local authorities. Previously most inmates had to be paid for by relatives. The original East House building was devoted to paying patients and the Western Department, completed in 1842, was reserved for the poorer admissions.

Dr McKinnon brought a new and more enlightened policy to the hospital and introduced many innovations. Wards fitted as dormitories now replaced the original solitary cells. He introduced musical concerts, excursions into the country, and religious services. Dr McKinnon's underlying principle was, as far as was feasible, to enable each patient to pursue the occupation he had followed in his everyday life and to make the hospital's environment as normal as possible, with facilities provided for carpentry, tailoring, shoe-making, basket-making, bookbinding, printing, and, for women, sewing, knitting, embroidery and domestic work. Gardening was encouraged. Apart from the value as "occupational therapy" of the above activities, they involved patients living in a somewhat independent community, also supplying self-supporting services, from the production of vegetables to maintenance and repair services of many kinds. A patient with former teaching experience taught more illiterate fellow-patients to read and write, which was beneficial both to him and to those he instructed. The installation of a printing-press coincided with the admission of a former newspaper editor, and in 1845 an asylum magazine was first published, *The Morningside Mirror*, with high quality contributions from patients and outside contributors; this continued to appear for nearly half a century.

Unveiling of Memorial to Dr Phillipe Pinel
with McKinnon House in background
By courtesy of the Royal Edinburgh Hospital

The old custodial and restraining approach of earlier days gave way to the community approach, in which Dr McKinnon was far ahead of his time. His appointment of a properly trained nursing matron, and steady improvement in staff training, brought what was originally an asylum to within sight of becoming "a therapeutic community". Unfortunately, Dr McKinnon's service at Morningside was relatively short-lived. While on a return visit to Aberdeen he died there, of typhus fever, on January 24th 1849, aged 34, and after only eight years in his Edinburgh post during which he had achieved so very much. He was buried in St Nicholas's Churchyard, Union Street, Aberdeen. The naming after him in recent years of the new bulding which he was appointed to inaugurate and in which he carried out so much enlightened work is a truly fitting memorial.

PHILIPPE PINEL

IN its early days the doctors in charge of the new mental hospital at Morningside were eager to learn all they might concerning the relatively new subject of psychiatry and its practical applications. Much pioneering work had been done in England by William Tuke of the Society of Friends (or Quakers) to whom, in 1792, he had appealed for funds to build "The Retreat", an early centre for psychiatric treatment in York. Edinburgh doctors went there to observe Tuke's methods. They had also heard of the quite revolutionary work being done by a French psychiatrist, Dr Philippe Pinel, in the Bicêtre Hospital in Paris. In 1819-20, the future distinguished Dr (later Sir) Robert Christison, Professor of Medical Jurisprudence at Edinburgh, and Dr Andrew Combe, physiologist and phrenologist, had attended University lectures delivered by Dr Esquirol, Pinel's assistant in the Salpêtrière in Paris, and then later met Pinel himself in his hospital wards.

Pinel was born in 1745 of humble background, educated at his village school, eventually graduating at Montpelier Medical School. The proper and more humane treatment of those considered insane was one of the many urgent reforms that were introduced following the French

Revolution in 1789, and Pinel became enthusiastically caught up in this. After considerable experience of working with mental illness in other hospitals and clinics he was appointed in charge of the Bicêtre Hospital. One of the first steps he took, and at the time and in the circumstances considered revolutionary and even dangerous, was the unchaining of the many patients who had been treated like animals. Pinel followed this with basic reforms such as much more suitable buildings, good food, warm clothing, and the treatment of inmates with dignity and respect. In collaboration with Dr Esquirol, he made important discoveries and introduced new forms of diagnosis and treatment.

In about 1840, when the new extension, the Western Department, now McKinnon House, of what had become known as the Royal Edinburgh Lunatic Asylum was opened, under Dr William McKinnon's charge, a bust of Pinel was placed over the main entrance way. This was the first memorial erected to Pinel anywhere, that in Paris not being unveiled until 1885, such was the Edinburgh psychiatrists' great respect for the French pioneer. However, when in 1930, other additions and alterations were made to the building, and its main entrance became situated at the rear, at the instigation of Professor George Robertson, Physician Superintendent, on September 26th a great gathering of nearly 250 people, medicals, officials, councillors, benefactors, interested people, witnessed the unveiling of a bronze bust of Pinel, similar to that in the Academy of Medicine in Paris, installed in a specially built monumental bay outside the east frontage of the then named West House, with six other medallions below Pinel, of people who had done much to advance the treatment of mental illness, including Dr Andrew Duncan. The occasion, a belated marking of the centenary of Pinel's death, was attended by the French Ambassador who unveiled the bust and addressed the assembly.

SIR HENRY JARDINE

MOST recent of the new facilities to be built at the Royal Edinburgh Hospital is the Jardine Clinic for psycho-geriatric patients, opened by Mr Magnus Magnusson in the autumn of 1982, providing 120 beds for inpatients and a 50 place day unit, with wards appropriately named Jordan, Canaan, Nile and Eden in Morningside's Biblical association context. Certainly the naming of the clinic after Sir Henry Jardine is most appropriate, since it was he who was responsible for obtaining the hospital's Royal Charter in 1807, two years before the foundation stone was laid.

Sir Henry Jardine was born on January 30th 1766, son of the Reverend Dr John Jardine, minister of Edinburgh's Tron Church, who was also one of the Deans of the Chapel Royal and of the Order of the Thistle. Sir Henry's mother was a daughter of the famous Lord Provost, George Drummond, who pioneered the building of the North Bridge, the development of the New Town, and the Royal Infirmary in the appropriately named Drummond Street. Qualified as a Writer to the Signet in 1790, Sir Henry Jardine

Sir Henry Jardine (8th from left)
with the Managers of the Edinburgh Orphan Hospital 1836
Silhouette reproduction by A. Edouart
By courtesy of the National Galleries of Scotland, Edinburgh

became Solicitor of Taxes for Scotland three years later. In 1794, he married Catherine, youngest daughter of George Skene of Rubislaw, Aberdeenshire. He obtained several high government posts, giving him influence which he used to obtain the Royal Charter for the new asylum about to be built at Morningside. He was knighted by George IV in 1825.

Amongst the public bodies of which Sir Henry Jardine was a member, and often a very active one, were the Royal Society of Edinburgh, the Society of Antiquaries of Scotland, the Scottish Naval and Military Academy, the Royal Company of Archers, and the Caledonian Horticultural Society — founded by Dr Andrew Duncan, responsible for the establishment of the new asylum. He was also involved in the management of the Orphan Hospital, which stood to the east of the North Bridge, near the former Trinity College Church, the Deaf and Dumb Institute, the House of Refuge, the Royal Infirmary and the Royal Public Dispensary — also founded by Dr Andrew Duncan. He died on August 11th 1851, aged 85. The naming of the new clinic after Sir Henry Jardine not only provides a fitting link with the past, with the era of Dr Andrew Duncan, but also with his own very considerable commitment to public service.

2 · CANAAN

THE largest of the "lots" or lands which resulted from the feuing out of the Burgh Muir in 1586 was Canaan, extending to sixty-five acres, its boundaries stretching almost to Blackford Avenue on the east, Morningside Road on the west, Newbattle Terrace and Grange Loan on the north and southwards to the Pow or Jordan Burn running past the old toll house at the foot of Morningside Road eastwards by Jordan Lane, Nile Grove, Blackford and Mayfield to its junction with the Braid Burn at Peffermill.

Over the centuries the Burgh Muir became largely cleared of its great trees to produce, in the 1800s, fine pasture land and garden ground with most pleasant, secluded, rural atmosphere. This, together with Canaan's size, resulted in a very large number of Edinburgh people, perhaps already with a house in the classical northern New Town or preferring to reside in the rural south, building themselves, or in summer renting, villas in Canaan. So secluded were so many of these houses that one writer described the residents of Canaan as "ensconced in their snug boxes".

Thus these delightful features of Canaan attracted especially writers, poets, artists, busy academics, distinguished medical men seeking respite from the bustle and pressures of life in the city or seeking inspiration for their art of authorship. So numerous and so varied in their achievements and interests were the people who from the early 1800s came to reside in Canaan that they would merit a separate book. Several were referred to in detail in an earlier volume and these with the many others are mostly and of necessity presented now with considerable brevity.

GEORGE MEIKLE KEMP

WITHIN Canaan, one of the most pleasant secluded leafy locations was the row of cottages and villas at Jordan Bank, whose often large gardens sloped gently downwards to the Jordan Burn. It was long ago renamed Jordan Lane, and is so known today, and here at No. 5 is Ainslie Cottage where for a short time resided George Meikle Kemp, architect of the Scott Monument. His death from accidental drowning in the canal occurred in March 1844 when he was returning to Ainslie Cottage from his office in the city, and his public funeral took place in St Cuthbert's churchyard.

Kemp was born in the small village of Moorfoot, near Gladhouse Loch on the border of Midlothian and Peebleshire. His father was a shepherd and the family frequently moved from place to place as work arose. Hence many schools in the area claim George Meikle Kemp as a former pupil. He served as an apprentice carpenter for five years at the little village of Redscourhead from the age of 14. Later he worked as a millwright at Galashiels, originally walking there and being given a lift on the road by Sir Walter Scott passing in his carriage, then not to know that his passenger would one day build his principal monument.

Kemp returned to Edinburgh and a post as a carpenter with John Cousin of Greenhill Gardens, builder

176

George Meikle Kemp

Showing Scott Monument under construction
by William Bonnar
By courtesy of the National Galleries of Scotland, Edinburgh

of many Edinburgh tenements, and he worked a ten-hour day. He then travelled widely on foot, in England and in Europe, sketching famous abbeys and other buildings. He returned to Edinburgh again and this time worked with the distinguished architect William Burn. Kemp's own ambitions in architecture had originally been inspired by a boyhood visit to Roslin chapel which impressed him deeply. He began submitting plans in architectural competitions for contracts. In 1836 the Edinburgh committee planning a fitting memorial to Sir Walter Scott invited designs. Kemp submitted one, above the *nom-de-plume* "John Morvo" the name of one of the stonemasons of Melrose Abbey which fascinated the aspiring architect. At first the committee made no award, then re-advertised

for another plan. Again Kemp submitted his entry. This time his design was chosen.

Many difficulties arose: money for the building of his projected monument was sparse. However, the foundation stone was laid by Lord Provost James Forrest of Comiston on August 15th 1840. Kemp worked ceaselessly on his commission, which also was his all-pervading dream. His tragic death occurred just as completion was in sight. This was effected by Kemp's brother-in-law, William Bonnar RSA by October 26th 1844. The son of the monument's creator was permitted to place the final top coping-stone in position. The cost was £15,000, and the monument is 200 feet 6 inches high, the top platform reached by 286 steps. Reaction to Kemp's creation was mixed and controversial, but praise from several noted architects and the Edinburgh sponsoring committee completely vindicated Kemp's design as a work of genius by a "culpably modest, diffident but lovable man". Kemp's friend James Ballantyne wrote a poem inscribed on the tombstone in St Cuthbert's churchyard, within sight of the Scott Monument:

Yet hope still cheers us while we mourn
And fame strews laurels o'er his urn.
Behold that structure cleave the sky,
And dream not genius e'er can die.

SAM BOUGH

FURTHER along Jordan Lane, at Jordan Bank Villa, originally 7 Jordan Bank, now 15 Jordan Lane, resided the celebrated landscape painter and lively Bohemian character Sam Bough, from 1867 until his death there on November 19th 1878.

Terrace, Edinburgh, and later to 2 Hill Street, and then, towards the end of 1867, to Jordan Bank. In what is now No 14 Jordan Lane, there is in the drawing-room a fine decorative ceiling which may have been the work of Sam Bough or predecessor in this house, David Hay, but at any rate Sam Bough carved his and his wife's initials in the ceiling cross-pieces. Although there is a large glass-enclosed verandah-type room to the rear of the house, since this faces south it is thought that Bough's studio was in a north-facing room in Jordan Bank Villa, No 15. He also had a studio at 2a George Street.

Of Bohemian appearance in dress, with a bluff, humorous and generous nature, he became a well-known character in Morningside, and a

Sam Bough

by Robert Anderson

By courtesy of the National Galleries of Scotland, Edinburgh

He also acquired the two adjacent houses, Nos 14 and 16. Sam Bough was born at Carlisle in 1822, son of a shoemaker, who encouraged his son's talent for sketching but arranged for his apprenticeship to a lawyer. To the future artist such work was uncongenial and he left Carlisle, for some time travelling with a group of gypsies in the Lake District. Without any formal training he nevertheless began painting pictures, which sold well. He acquired work as a scenery painter in Manchester and then in Glasgow, where he remained for seven years. This theatrical experience is said to be obvious in the minute and often dramatic detail of much of his landscape work. In 1866 he moved from Glasgow to 5 Malta

Sam Bough

Photograph possibly taken in his garden at Jordan Bank

By courtesy of Watson Kerr

178

regular customer at the "Volunteer's Rest", for which he painted two sign-boards. Robert Louis Stevenson may well have visited Sam Bough at Jordan Bank for they became close friends. Bough was elected a member of the Royal Scottish Academy in 1875. His prolific landscapes were mainly of Scottish or north-of-England scenes, especially bustling harbours and secluded bays, which fascinated him. Most of his work is now in private collections and at public auction can command a high price. Glasgow Art Gallery has several examples of his work. Caw, the authority on Scottish artists, wrote that in his time Sam Bough was the most popular landscape painter in Scotland — more popular even than McTaggart. A number of portraits and statuettes of Bough himself exist. Apparently he was not an admirer of David Octavius Hill's famous and otherwise highly praised Disruption painting, the result of painstaking work over very many years and combining early photo-graphy and portrait painting of the four hundred ministers signing the Disruption Deed of Demission.

Bough compared the grouping of the portraits to "Potatoes all in a row". Apart from having an eye for copious detail in his landscapes, the artist apparently also possessed a quite phenomenal memory and could commit many pages to mind and readily recite these aloud to a group of friends. He died at Jordan Bank on November 19th 1878, aged 56, and was buried in Dean Cemetery.

DAVID RAMSAY HAY

SAM BOUGH, relates his biographer,

David Ramsay Hay

with his dog "Brush"
By courtesy of Mr Ian Gow

had carried out some interior decora-tion at Jordan Bank Villa before taking up residence in 1867, six months after the death there of its previous owner, who has been described as "The First Intellectual House-painter". This was David Ramsay Hay. Hay was born in Edin-burgh in March 1798. His father, a banker and proprietor of the *Edin-burgh Evening Courant*, provided for his early education, and then had him placed in a printing office as a "reading boy" but died soon after arranging this. David Hay found the work most uncongenial and much preferred drawing. (Shades of his successor Sam Bough!) Hay found employment with Gavin Beugo, a

179

heraldic and decorative painter in Edinburgh, and was encouraged to pursue his special interest — the painting of animals.

Some of Hay's work attracted the attention of Sir Walter Scott, especially his portrait of Scott's favourite cat! Scott encouragéd him to make a career of house painting, not only as "a useful service to the mass of the people", but which could also be practised at a high artistic level. In token of his high opinion of his work Scott employed Hay in the decoration of Abbotsford. By 1828 Hay was firmly established in business with his partner George Nicholson in George Street, and from then onwards obtained numerous contracts for high-class interior decoration, including work on certain of the baroque features of Holyrood Palace, from Queen Victoria, in 1850, and also at Mortonhall House.

Hay wrote much on the theory and practice of the fine arts, his first work on *Laws of Harmonious Colouring* and other studies on the application of mathematics (especially geometry), to design in interior decoration, is said to have pioneered the rendering of "imitation damask". He moved in Edinburgh's intellectual and cultural circles and was regarded as a fine product of the city's Age of Enlightenment. Hay was a founder member of the Aesthetic Society, whose members included Professors Kelland, Goodsir, James Y. Simpson and Dr John Brown, author of *Rab and His Friends.* He was awarded a special medal from the Royal Scottish Society of Arts for the invention of a machine which could draw the perfect egg oval or "composite

ellipse". Hay was said to have set the tone in house decoration for the remainder of the 19th century. He died at Jordan Bank Villa on September 10th 1866.

HENRY KINGSLEY

LEAVING Jordan Lane, one of Morningside's many Biblical names, and entering Canaan Lane from Morningside Road, such names are now constantly encountered and, almost literally, every few yards there arise associations with people of interest. Only a short distance along on the right a plaque on an old-world cottage-type house indicates "Goshen", and a few yards further on beyond the most recent little group of houses, "The Hamlet", a

Henry Kingsley

Visiting card portrait by Mason
By courtesy of the National Portrait Gallery, London

180

little back from the street and partially hidden behind another two cottages, stands "Goshen Bank", the largest and principal house in this Biblical location, with its main entrance to the rear facing south and once entered from what was Jordan Bank. Here in October 1869 came to reside Henry Kingsley, after his appointment as editor of the *Edinburgh Daily Review*, a penny daily newspaper published by the Free Presbyterian Church and with some Scottish Episcopalian support. This post marked what was virtually the penultimate stage in Kingsley's rather sad and tragic life.

Born in Barnack in Northamptonshire on January 2nd 1830, Henry Kingsley was the third son of the Reverend Henry Kingsley and the younger brother of the much more celebrated Charles Kingsley, author of *Westward Ho!* and *The Water Babies.* Somewhat reminiscent of Charles Chalmers, Henry spent a great deal of his life, as previously mentioned, cast in an inferior position under the shadow of his more famous elder brother. Henry Kingsley left Worcester College, Oxford, in 1853, having enjoyed the university's social life and having been a successful rower, but having failed to gain a degree. He set out with friends for the Australian goldfields. There he spent four unsuccessful years, but on his return to England his novel *The Recollections of Geoffrey Hamly*, drawn from his Australian experiences, brought considerable attention and started him on a writing career which was destined to fluctuate between success and failure. He wrote twenty-four books and very many essays, articles and short stories, but whatever his financial gains his apparent irresponsibility in household expenditure and his rather erratic life style, coupled with ill-health, led to the verge of bankruptcy, to much tension and domestic unhappiness.

Kingsley married his second cousin, Sarah Maria Kingsley, and settled in Wargrave near Henley-on-Thames. His taking up of the editorship of the *Edinburgh Daily Review* and removal to Morningside with his wife was an attempt to achieve some financial stability. He published a great deal of his own work in the *Review*, and contributions from his wife on Edinburgh issues of the day, but he was not considered successful, one critic describing him as "a round man in a square hole". At Goshen Bank, the Kingsleys were visited by Ann Thackeray. In 1870 he took on the assignment as the *Review's* correspondent in the Franco-Prussian War, basing himself at Metz, again in search of pecuniary improvement.

Kingsley returned to Edinburgh but lost his post with the *Review* in April 1871, and a month later returned to London. He attempted other novels but against failing health, and returned to Cuckfield, in Sussex, where he died of cancer of the tongue after a brief illness on May 24th 1876. Almost a century after Henry Kingsley's death Dr J. S. D. Mellick, of the Department of English Literature, Queensland University, Australia, researching for the subsequent publication of a scholarly biography of Kingsley, *The Passing Guest*, called upon Mr Wilfred Taylor and myself and together we visited Goshen Bank. Dr Mellick took a photograph which appears in his book.

WILLIAM RITCHIE

William Ritchie

A FEW yards eastwards beyond Goshen Bank, at 34 Canaan Lane, is yet another Biblical name, "Hebron Bank". Here in this house in 1832 there resided William Ritchie, one of the co-founders of *The Scotsman*, his partner being Charles Maclaren who, though also a "Canaanite", lived much further eastwards in the large villa called "Morelands", today part of the Astley Ainslie Hospital and situated at its eastern gateway in Whitehouse Terrace.

William Ritchie was born in 1781 in the village of Lundin Mill in Fife, his father being engaged in the flax-dressing industry. At the age of 19 Ritchie came to Edinburgh as an apprentice in a solicitor's office. In 1808 he became a member of the Society of Solicitors before the Supreme Court and soon established his own successful firm. He began contributing articles to the *Scots Magazine* and other publications and had plans for producing a *Biographia Scotica*, but this he abandoned. As he had entered the field of newspapers and journals, Ritchie had begun to notice in the Edinburgh publications, of which there were many, an unwillingness to print anything which was critical of "the Establishment", whether the Town Council or other public bodies. This offended his sense of fairness and openness to the truth. In 1816 matters came to a head when the local newspapers rejected certain criticisms he had submitted concerning the management of the Royal Infirmary. His friend, Charles Maclaren, shared his indignation at what they considered the suppression of the facts and a lack of impartiality. Together, they made an extremely bold decision: to found another newspaper, "come what may". It would be impartial, of independent mind, although it would advocate Liberal reforms. Maclaren wrote of his friend: "He assisted in forming the plan, suggested the title, drew up the prospectus, and by his exertion and personal influence did more than any other individual to establish the paper".

The first number of *The Scotsman* appeared on January 25th 1817. Ritchie wrote the "Preliminary Note" and three other articles. The new paper was published weekly at ten pence. In 1823 it appeared bi-weekly at seven pence, then eventually, in 1855, daily. Charles Maclaren, who had a high position in the Customs and Excise service, concentrated, as joint editor, on political affairs, in which he was well informed; also scientific matters and technology. Ritchie wrote on legal questions, fine arts, and theatre, literature, moral and metaphysical issues. It was calculated that during his fourteen years' association with *The Scotsman*, Ritchie wrote 1,000 articles, "embracing such a mass of writing as to fill twenty or thirty closely printed octavo volumes". Through him, it was said, public opinion in the country had made a great advance, "was more independent, more readily expressed, more articulate". Maclaren said of his friend: "It often struck me as remarkable that in Ritchie's character so much force was combined with so much tenderness, and that one who was so much the creature of impulse should have had so much consideration for the feelings of others". It was agreed that Ritchie by his "campaigning articles" and other efforts had been instrumental in improving the police system, ameliorating prison discipline, establishing in Edinburgh a House of Refuge and a society for the relief of poor debtors. William Ritchie died on February 4th 1831, aged 50, and was buried in Greyfriars churchyard. John, his elder brother, who had become a successful draper in Edinburgh, assisted financially in the establishment of *The Scotsman* and in many other ways.

ELIZA FLETCHER

LOOKING down Woodburn Terrace from its junction with Canaan Lane the meeting-place of Nile Grove and Braid Avenue can be seen. This is the lowest point in Morningside and along this gentle valley flows the Jordan Burn, mainly underground, from west to east. On the burn's southern bank at this point was the location known as Egypt and referred

Mrs Eliza Fletcher

(née Eliza Dawson at age 15)
Engraving by James Faed
From "Autobiography of Mrs E. Fletcher"

to in the Burgh Records for 1585 when Rovert Fairlie, Laird of Braid (the latter estate's northern boundary was the Jordan Burn), had granted the city "the use of his houses callit Littil Egypt besyde the common mure for the brewing thairin of the drink for the seik folkis in the mure ...". This is the earliest occurrence of a Biblical or eastern name in the Morningside area, and it is known from other sources also as "Littil Egypt". The use of the word "Littil" especially as so spelt, strongly suggests the existence on the location referred to above of a gypsy colony, whose members, having fallen foul of the local authorities in many parts of Scotland in the mid 16th-century, were forced to leave the cities. In the case of Edinburgh, to comply with this decree, the gypsies simply needed

183

literally to step across the Jordan Burn and into the lands of Braid and they were outwith the city. Hence the origin in Braid of "Littil Egypt". At any rate, while in succeeding centuries many Biblical names appeared in the district such as Canaan, Eden, Goshen and others, which still remain known as such, Egypt began to be less known locally at the end of the 19th century, when the large farm of that name which for long had extended southwards from the corner of Nile Grove and Braid Avenue, came to be built upon and lost to memory.

A local street has now been named "Egypt Mews".

While little is known concerning Egypt Farm save its appearance on old maps, especially Charles Gordon's "Plan of the Barony of Braid" of 1772, and its mention as a fare stage for the early hackney coaches plying out from the city, the names of two families who resided at Egypt Farm have come to light. In the autobiography of Mrs Eliza Fletcher, an English lady, wife of a noted Edinburgh advocate, published in 1875, there is this entry: "In the summer of 1799, during the vacation of the courts, Mr Fletcher's health, as well as my own, seeming to require a change of air, we repaired with our children to a very inexpensive cottage in the Morningside district to the south of Edinburgh called Egypt — so named in memory of a gypsy colony, who, as tradition said, had made their headquarters in the immediate whereabouts by virtue of a grant of land given to them by one of the Scottish Kings. . . ."

Mrs Eliza Fletcher was of the Dawson family of Tadcaster in York-shire. While aged only 17 she was introduced to a notable Edinburgh advocate, Archibald Fletcher, who was "aged about 43 and of a grave, gentlemanly, prepossessing appearance". Her father opposed the marriage, preferring her to wed a titled gentleman, but on July 16th 1791 she married Fletcher in Tadcaster Church. Archibald Fletcher was born in Glenlyon in Perthshire and educated at Kenmore, Perth and Edinburgh. Apprenticed to a Writer to the Signet in Edinburgh he attended certain University classes. He was a fellow student and close friend of Dugald Stewart and later of Henry Erskine. He was called to the Scottish Bar in 1790. Deeply sympathetic to the French Revolution, he attended the Bastille celebrations every year. He was much involved in the local government system of his time.

In Edinburgh the Fletchers were close friends of the celebrated Dr William Cullen of the Medical School, whose home was the focal point for most of the prominent literary figures of the city — David Hume, Adam Smith, Joseph Black and Henry McKenzie. In the spring of 1794 Mrs Fletcher's father, obviously reconciled to her marriage, bought her a house at 20 Queen Street. Mrs Fletcher became a great friend of the prominent Edinburgh lady, Joanna Baillie. In April 1824 the family moved to Auchendinny House, "an old and odd-looking *château* on the North Esk", previously the residence of Henry McKenzie. Here they were visited by Sydney Smith. Mr Archibald Fletcher died at Auchendinny House on December 20th 1828. Mrs Fletcher died at Lancrigg nearly thirty years later. She was buried in the graveyard of Grasmere Parish Church, and there is a stone carved memorial to her inside the church.

The only other family discovered on record as having resided at Egypt Farm, and this quite by chance by a friend visiting Grange Cemetery and seeing the headstone — were named Begbie. The stone is inscribed: "In memory of John Begbie, Egypt Farm, Morningside. Died 29th November 1881 aged 65". Other members of the family are in the same grave. Sam Bough, while living at Jordan Bank Villa in Jordan Lane, refers to his climbing a low wall at the foot of his garden, crossing the Jordan Burn and going into "Mr Begbie's field at Egypt Farm". This was about 1870.

Mrs Eliza Fletcher: aged 80

Engraved by James Faed from drawing by Benze Richmond
From "Autobiography of Mrs E. Fletcher"

GEORGE ROSS

ONE man who earned a prominent and important place in the annals of Morningside was George Ross of Woodburn House in Canaan Lane. He played a leading part in the raising of funds for the establishment of the parish church, but perhaps his major contribution to the life of early Morningside was as one of the original four sponsors of the Old School-house which opened in 1823. George Ross, an advocate of some note and later a Judge of the Commissary Court of Scotland, was in 1810 one of the trustees of the Rose Street Industrial School founded by Lady Maxwell of Pollock shortly before her death in the same year. The charter of 1823 by which William Deuchar, the then owner of Morningside estate, conveyed the small portion of land required for the building of the school-house, names the four men who planned to open the little village school, and the first named is George Ross of Woodburn House. One of the others was Alexander Falconar of Falcon Hall; the third, James Evans of Canaan Park; and the fourth, Henry Hare, who appears to have resided outwith Morningside.

In 1856, when the school-house had been functioning for thirty-three years, George Ross "settled" £1,300, apparently of his own money, for its continuation, recording that he had retained its management. There were several other trustees. It would appear that this exclusive personal support by Ross led to the name "The Ross School' and later, when fees were levied on parents who could afford to pay, "The Subscription School". As with a number of

The Wee School, Morningside

Morningside Old Schoolhouse

For long known as the Ross Subscription School

people who played an important part in the development of South Edinburgh, or certainly merit inclusion in its chronicles on account of their achievements in various spheres, much more is known about what they did than about them personally. Unfortunately George Ross is another case in point. Woodburn House was built in 1812, and George Ross appears to have lived there from 1818 until his death in 1861. Born on October 25th 1775, he was the third son of Admiral Sir John Lockhart Ross of Balnagowan. In June 1808 he married Grace, daughter of the Reverend Andrew Hunter of Barjarg. He was an Advocate-Depute from 1803-6 and appointed a Judge of the Commissary Court in 1813. George Ross's youngest son, George Lockhart Ross, born in July 1814, became Professor of Scots Law in Edinburgh University from 1862 until his early death from diphtheria a year later.

SIR FRANK MEARS

RESIDENT in Woodburn House for some years from 1914 was Sir Frank Mears, a noted architect, but most distinguished perhaps as one of the leading town planners of modern times. His survey and plan for the Forth Region, drawn up during the Second World War, was a pioneering work in the field of regional studies. Frank Mears was born in Tynemouth in 1880 and when his family came to Edinburgh he attended George Watson's College. He received architectural training from Hippolyte Blanc and attended the Edinburgh School of Art. In the First World War, as a captain in the Royal Flying Corps Kite Balloon Service, he invented "The Mears Parachute". Resuming civilian work he became associated with the famous Sir Patrick Geddes, founder of modern town and country planning, fell very much under his influence, specialised in this field and was awarded the Royal Institute of British Architects'

Sir Frank Mears

Reproduced from "The Scottish Arts Club, Edinburgh, 1874-1974"

By kind permission of the Scottish Arts Club

Distinction in Town Planning. He married Sir Patrick Geddes' daughter. Sir Frank Mears was President of the Royal Scottish Academy from 1944-50, a Fellow of the Royal Society of Edinburgh, and was awarded a knighthood in 1946.

Mears' father was Dr William Mears, a lecturer in anatomy, and his mother, Isabella Bartholomew, a member of the celebrated family of cartographers, was one of the earliest female graduates in medicine. Sir Patrick Geddes and Sir Frank Mears collaborated on many projects. One of special interest was the Royal Zoological Park at Corstorphine in which they introduced rock formations instead of concrete compounds. Their Edinburgh survey of 1908 stressed the relationships between history, people and country-side, also between architecture and the business enterprise involved. After the First World War their plans for the University and National Library at Jerusalem were thwarted when the authorities decided to employ a Jewish architect.

Sir Frank Mears was criticised by many as being unduly humble and subdued in manner, and in his work: it was said these characteristics prevented him from creating the best impression and reaching his full potential. The unpretentious David Livingstone memorial at Blantyre and the Lucy Sanderson homes at Galashiels gave him great joy. His restoration of Huntly House as Edinburgh's City Museum, and of Gladstone's Land, are considered characteristically unassuming but faultless in taste. His bridges in the north of Scotland have been rated as unsurpassed. The modern trend in the buildings of his day he lamented, describing much of it as "packing case in style". Perhaps Sir Frank Mears' love of the past, and especially his admiration for Scotland's sturdy castles, was expressed in what has been suggested as his most fitting memorial, the houses he created for the historical parts of Stirling, "mystically uniting the work-a-day present with the drama of Scotland's past". Sir Frank died on January 25th 1953, aged 73, while in Christ-church, New Zealand, visiting his son. Something of the co-founder's influence remains in the firm of architects, planning and landscape consultants of today, which still bears his name.

PROFESSOR JAMES GREGORY

Professor James Gregory
by Henry Raeburn
By courtesy of the National Galleries of Scotland, Edinburgh

AT the time of writing the face of Canaan is changing. The age-old open rural green spaces, amid stately trees, which attracted those seeking respite from a busy professional life or inspiration in literature or the arts, are now being built upon, and the trees cut down. Canaan Lodge, rebuilt in 1907, is nevertheless still associated with the most celebrated owner of the original villa, built in 1800. This was Professor James Gregory, immortalised at least among the present "older generation" for the famous mixture which bore his name. The amused smiles that greet the mention of that name seemingly for ever reminiscent of his celebrated remedy for digestive disorders, has tended to obscure recognition of the academic distinction of its creator.

Professor James Gregory, who acquired Canaan Lodge in 1814, was described as the last of "the Academic Gregorys", a remarkable Aberdeenshire family of whom fourteen held University professorial chairs within a period extending over two centuries. When he was appointed Professor of Medicine at Edinburgh University in 1776, aged only 23, he was the fifth of the Gregory family to hold an Edinburgh professorship. A man of boundless energy, he was reputedly a brilliant teacher whose popular classes acquired a constantly increasing membership that was unprecedented. He succeeded the highly distinguished Professor William Cullen and became the dominant influence in the Edinburgh Medical School during its heyday of world-wide renown; he also established the leading consultancy practice in Scotland.

The production of Gregory's Mixture involved another Morningside resident and medical man, Dr Thomas Steel and a friend whose stately home was much further east, Sir Alexander Dick of Prestonfield House. The formula included magnesia, pulverised rhubarb and ginger. The magnesia Dr Steel mass-produced at his factory on the western boundary of Canaan at what is now commemoratively known as Steel's Place. The rhubarb Sir Alexander Dick, who was President of the Royal College of Physicians, grew in large crops at Prestonfield; he was probably the first to cultivate it in Scotland, where the soil was particularly suitable, having been richly fertilised over many years by the action of Sir Alexander's father who, when Lord Provost of Edinburgh, had had cartloads of horse manure from the city street sweepings brought out and dumped on the Prestonfield land. Professor James Gregory was a man of very wide cultural interests, a distinguished Latin scholar, a powerful controversialist, moving in Edinburgh's leading intellectual circles and constantly attracting distinguished adherents. He died in April 1821, aged 65, and was buried in Canongate churchyard. His son became Professor of Chemistry at Edinburgh University.

KING JAMIE THE FOURTH

WHILE the Kings and Queens of Scotland regularly rode or were conveyed between Edinburgh Castle and Holyrood or elsewhere around or outside the city, it is known for certain that on at least one occasion,

James IV, King of Scotland (1488-1513)

the rather rudimentary cottages of the people working steadily to bring the rough and overgrown Burgh Muir under cultivation and suitable for cattle, as first begun nearly three centuries earlier by the monks at the Grange of St Giles. To this whole peaceful rural scene, so full of hope, as elsewhere in Scotland and especially in the Borders, might well be applied the lines of Mrs Jane Elliot's famous and moving lament, *The Flowers of the Forest*:

> I've heard them lilting, at our ewe-milking,
> Lasses a-lilting, before the dawn of day;
> But now they are moaning, on ilka green loaning;
> The Flowers of the Forest are a' wede away.

JOHN BEUGO

in November 1507, James IV rode beyond its boundaries and visited the small chapel of St Roque (or Roch) out on the Burgh Muir, which in fact he may himself have built. The site may still be pointed out within the pleasant grounds of the Astley Ainslie Hospital.

In his dramatic poem *Marmion* Sir Walter Scott describes the Scottish army, if not in fact the 100,000 which Marmion saw, certainly as many thousands mustered in the same area around St Roque's in August 1513 prior to their departure for the disastrous Flodden Field. Scott describes also James reviewing his army while there encamped. There is some evidence that a gypsy colony existed near to St Roque's in the early 16th century and possibly there were

John Beugo
by George Willison
By courtesy of the National Galleries of Scotland, Edinburgh

189

CONSIDERABLE interest remains, and indeed seems to have increased, in the chapel of St Roque (or Roch), built out on the isolated Burgh Muir. Around it wooden huts were built to house the thousands of "seik folkis" suffering from "the peste" (Black Death) which invaded Edinburgh at intervals from early centuries until the last reported outbreak in 1645, one of the most severe ever recorded. St Roque was venerated in Europe as the patron saint of the plague-stricken, and it was James IV's devotion to him which prompted the foundation of the chapel, along with others in Glasgow and elsewhere in Scotland, in the hope that the victims quarantined in their vicinity would, through the prayers of the permanent chaplain attached, recover their health.

Many ancient ecclesiastical stones have been found in the Astley Ainslie grounds and in the gardens of nearby villas in Canaan, originally believed to have come from the ruins of St Roque's; but now, as the result of research, it seems more likely that the stones may have emanated from the famous church of the Holy Trinity, demolished to make way for the building of the Waverley Station in 1848, or during the various restorations of St Giles, and were brought out to the Canaan district. At least three illustrations of the little chapel of St Roque are extant, showing it in a state of ruin, one an engraving by J. Hooper of 1789, reproduced in *Grose's Antiquities*, another by Sparrow, undated, and a third by the noted engraver John Beugo (1759-1841), which appeared in *Poems on Various Subjects* by James Macaulay, published in 1888. These illustrations are of value in research on the origin of the Canaan stones. Beugo was an engraver noted, perhaps, for his reproduction in stipple of Robert Burns by Alexander Nasmyth, the poet having given Beugo several sittings. The engraver himself also wrote poetry. The first notes of the Commercial Bank of Scotland were the work of Beugo in 1810-11. John Beugo was born in Edinburgh on May 7th 1759 and died on December 13th 1841. St Roque's was not finally demolished until 1791, so that Beugo would have been able to visit it even before it was completely ruined, and therefore his illustration is of real significance.

PROFESSOR JAMES SYME

Professor James Syme: aged 65

From "Memorials of the Life of James Syme"
by Robert Paterson, M.D.

CANAAN not only attracted architects, writers and poets, but also became very much a "medical quarter". If Professor James Gregory of Canaan Lodge earned the highest reputation as a physician, some twenty years later Canaan attracted another highly distinguished medical man, Professor James Syme, described as "the Napoleon of Surgery", who acquired the villa "Millbank" in what are now the grounds of the Astley Ainslie Hospital and indeed on whose site a hospital pavilion stands commemoratively named "Millbank". Until a few years ago, although "Millbank" villa had long since been demolished, its kitchen garden remained and also parts of Syme's once beloved greenhouses. All this was cleared away for the building of the fine large and well-furnished geriatric day hospital, the Balfour Pavilion. Three famous medical names are almost inseparably linked with the former villa of "Millbank", and since each has been the subject of biographies only brief mention is made here.

Professor Syme was born at 56 Princes Street on November 7th 1799. While still attending Edinburgh's High School and spending his spare time in what was a university extra-mural chemistry laboratory in Lothian Street, with which Dr John Deuchar of Morningside House was associated as a lecturer, young James Syme discovered a solvent for rubber and a process for impregnating cloth with the solution to render it waterproof. He published his discovery but, stating that the ethics of his future profession in medicine precluded him, he did not commercially exploit his process. This was done by Charles Macintosh of Glasgow, a manufacturing chemist, who developed Syme's method, patented it and made a fortune. The raincoat which he produced bearing his name became a household word.

After qualifying in medicine Syme became a demonstrator in anatomy, and was in charge of the city's small fever hospital beside the old Royal Infirmary before studying for some time in Europe. Returning to Edinburgh about 1825 he lectured in anatomy and later surgery. By 1829 Syme's apparently difficult personality led to a vendetta with Dr Robert Liston and lost him a Royal Infirmary appointment. Indeed this difficulty in relating amicably to colleagues was a constant problem and especially with the famous Professor J. Y. Simpson, pioneer of chloroform. Undaunted by the Royal Infirmary rejection, Syme opened his own private surgical hospital in Minto House in what became Chambers Street. This hospital, and its atmosphere, was to be immortalised by Syme's assistant there, Dr John Brown, in his classic story, *Rab and his Friends.* Brown, who knew Syme "at close quarters", paid unstinting tribute to "the Chief", his brilliance and skill, commenting that "he never wasted a word, a drop of ink or a drop of blood". Syme was much involved in the passing of the Medical Act of 1858 and the setting up of the General Medical Council.

With a life involved in so much controversy and personal rivalries, often of his own making, and of course his demanding surgical duties, Syme found welcome respite in returning in the evenings to his secluded villa at Millbank which he had acquired in 1842. There in his large greenhouses he delighted in cultivating all sorts of exotic plants and fruits. He was often consulted at Millbank by notable patients, such as Charles Dickens while in Edinburgh to deliver a recital of readings from his work, and Thomas Carlyle during his visit to be installed as Rector of the University in 1866, and upon whom Syme performed a minor operation, the patient convalescing at Millbank. Whatever his problems in relating amicably with many of his medical colleagues, there was one, destined to become much more famous than himself, with whom there developed an immediate rapport, the deepest respect, a close friendship, and who was to marry his daughter. This was the then young surgeon Joseph Lister.

LORD LISTER

JOSEPH LISTER was born in Essex in 1827 of very devout Quaker parents and graduated in medicine at University College, London. In the course of his post-graduate surgical training and after studying in Europe, he was advised to attend Syme's lectures in Edinburgh — "the most original and thoughtful surgeon in Europe". Lister arrived in Edinburgh in September 1853, obtained lodgings in Frederick Street and duly presented himself to Syme with an introductory letter from the latter's great friend in London, Professor Sharpey. Lister had intended staying in Edinburgh for one month but so impressed was he by Syme's lectures and surgical demonstrations and Edinburgh's medical training facilities that he remained rather longer, until in quite exceptional and

favoured circumstances he was appointed Syme's house surgeon in the old Royal Infirmary in January 1854.

Lister's surgical career, and especially his research into antiseptic surgery and his struggle to vindicate his revolutionary new techniques, while partly begun in Edinburgh, was greatly facilitated only after he became Professor of Surgery in Glasgow in 1860. His sensational results, rather like those of Professor James Simpson with chloroform, became part of popular history. As his personal friendship with Syme deepened, Lister would have been a frequent visitor to "Millbank" and there he met one of Syme's two daughters by his first marriage, Agnes. Joseph Lister and Agnes Syme were married in "Millbank" on April 23rd 1856. In view of the

Wedding photograph of Joseph Lister and Agnes Syme at Millbank, Canaan

devout Quakerism of Lister's relations, equalled by the ardent Episcopalianism of Syme's family, the Syme home was chosen rather than a church for the wedding ceremony, with both denominational officials participating. The first Lister home was at 11 Rutland Street, where a commemorative plaque remains. The honeymoon involved a tour of Europe with visits to many medical centres. Four years after his marriage and resumption of his work in Edinburgh, a vacancy occurred for the Regius Chair of Surgery in Glasgow. Lister was one of seven candidates. There was much lobbying but he was successful and appointed on January 28th 1860.

In 1869 the great Syme, who was almost seventy, was afflicted by recurring ill-health and he was forced to resign his Edinburgh Chair of Clinical Surgery. He nominated Lister as his successor. Again in the face of much competition Lister was appointed to succeed his father-in-law. Syme died following a second stroke at his home at "Millbank" on June 26th 1870. Lister, who continued his antiseptic surgery experiments in Edinburgh, eventually returned to London to propagate his new techniques. In the New Year Honours List of 1897 he was awarded a baronetcy, the first medical man in Britain to be so elevated. The honour vindicated his long struggle for the introduction of life-saving antiseptic techniques in surgery. Perhaps among the most cherished moments of his life were his several meetings with Louis Pasteur, whose own new teachings Lister had sought to apply to surgery. In the Old College of Edinburgh University there is a display case of the almost

innumerable awards of the highest distinction bestowed upon Lister by many nations. He died on February 10th 1912, aged 85. Lady Lister had predeceased him by nearly twenty years. They had no family.

DR JOHN BROWN

Lesser known portrait of Dr John Brown at Ambleside 1866

From "The Letters of Dr John Brown"

IT is significant that the congratulatory address at the wedding of Lister and Agnes Syme at "Millbank" was given by Dr John Brown, since he was one of the family's closest friends, a frequent and most welcome visitor to the Canaan villa. Nearly thirty years before, Brown, commencing his medical studies, had become apprenticed to Syme — at a very high fee, he once remarked — at his private surgical hospital at Minto House. Brown's literary classic, *Rab and His*

Friends, was still to be written three years later and was a vivid and eloquent recollection of a day in the life of the busy hospital. This was not Brown's only excursion into literature, and while he did publish much else, principally essays, and gain very great success, he remained primarily a physician, having eventually changed from surgery, with a remarkable humanitarianism and charisma, such that in his latter days his patients prevailed upon him not to retire.

Dr John Brown was born on September 22nd 1810 at Biggar where his father, a Biblical scholar, was minister of the Free Church before moving to Edinburgh. The boy's early education was gained from his father and sound enough to enable him to fit into Edinburgh High School's appropriate age group. He began studying medicine in 1828, at the formal courses, and training under Professor Syme at Minto House hospital. After a short period of experience at Chatham, dealing with cholera epidemics aboard ships, he returned to Edinburgh in 1833, gained his M.D. and exchanged surgery for general practice. His residence was at No 23 Rutland Street, then the "Harley Street" of Edinburgh. Syme's consulting rooms were at No 3, and Lister after his marriage resided at No 11.

Dr John Brown has been described as "Scotland's Charles Lamb". His first publication was his *Horae Subsecivae* (or *Leisure Hours*) a collection of essays, published in 1858, with two subsequent volumes in 1861 and 1882. *Rab and His Friends*, originally prepared as a lecture, entitled *The Howgate Carrier, His Wife and His Dog Rab*, and delivered at Biggar, first appeared in *Horae Subsecivae* in 1861, later as a pamphlet, then as a book. It sold 50,000 copies in four years. Brown has recounted how he wrote it straight off in four hours, commencing at midnight, retiring to bed "happy but cold". Robert Louis Stevenson wrote of it and its author:

. . . didna fash himself to think —
Ye stapped yer pen into the ink
And there was *Rab*

Pet Marjorie, of which 150,000 copies were sold soon after publication, has since caused questions to be raised concerning the authenticity of the events upon which Brown based his story. *Our Dogs* was another success. The illustrations in much of Brown's work were by Morningside artist Miss Hannah Preston Macgoun of Banner Lodge, near Church Hill. Brown was a close friend of Ruskin, Mark Twain and Thomas Carlyle, and indeed provides an interesting account of the latter's stay at "Millbank" when Syme operated on him. He used his wide circle of friends to the advantage of others who were seeking support or assistance. Although he produced much literature, Dr Brown always claimed that he was primarily a medical man, and indeed much of his writing illustrates his constant theme: that of the need for a doctor or surgeon to have a wide culture and humanitarian, if not Christian, background in approaching each patient as an individual; and while welcoming to a certain degree what he sometimes described as "the intrusion of science" into medicine, he argued that medicine must always remain primarily an art.

ALEXANDER JAMES ADIE

ARCHITECTURE, painting, journalism, surgery, were all among the various professions and skills represented by those who resided in the relatively small confines of that part of Canaan which became the grounds of the Astley Ainslie Hospital and the various private villas also eventually acquired by the hospital. The range of skills was further extended in about 1815 with the occupancy of Canaan Cottage by Alexander James Adie who acquired a high reputation as an optician, optical instrument maker and early manufacturer of thermometers, theodolites and barometers, which he produced and experimented upon in his house in Canaan.

Alexander James Adie was born in Edinburgh in 1775, and following his father's early death was looked after by his uncle, John Miller, an optician in Edinburgh and a man of broad learning who imbued his young nephew with an early taste for scholarship and scientific invention. Young Alexander Adie, too, took up optical work. Aware of his

Dr John Brown

By Sir George Reid
By courtesy of the National Galleries of Scotland, Edinburgh

Dr Brown was elected a Fellow of the Royal Society of Edinburgh in 1859 and awarded an LL.D. by Edinburgh University in 1874. Apart from his benign figure being a familiar and welcome sight in Canaan on his way to "Millbank", he also regularly visited Morningside Place where his sisters resided at No 7. He died on May 11th 1882 and is buried in New Calton Cemetery. On his death Swinburne wrote of him as having gone to:

> Some happier isle in the Elysian Sea
> Where Rab may lick the hand of
> Marjorie

Canaan Cottage
One-time home of Alexander James Adie
Photograph by W. R. Smith

195

inadequate early education he attended classes in his spare time. Soon his own inventive mind and technical efficiency brought him employment by other inventors seeking to give their ideas practical form. He became intensely interested in meteorology and set up a small observatory in a second house which he obtained in another part of Edinburgh, long before a public observatory was opened. One of his first inventions was the sympiesometer or marine barometer, of great value as regards the safety of shipping. Later, he assisted the distinguished Sir David Brewster in the construction of minute but powerful lenses used in microscopy. Gardening was as much a source of experimentation for him as a hobby. He was elected a Fellow of the Royal Society of Edinburgh in 1819.

In 1800, at the age of 25, he had taken over the optician's business of his uncle, moving to 94 Nicholson Street in 1804. Mainly on account of his service to inventors and scientists, his business became the most successful of its kind in Edinburgh. In 1830, employing his brother as an assistant, he moved to 58 Princes Street. Some years later he was appointed optician to King William IV and then to Queen Victoria. After residing in other parts of Edinburgh he returned to Canaan Cottage in the 1850s, where he died in 1859. Various other members of the Adie family continued in similar spheres of work. Canaan Cottage, shown in Kirkwood's map of 1817, but misspelt as "Mr Edie's Property", became the administrative centre of the Astley Ainslie Hospital.

Sympiesometer: invented by Adie

Photograph by courtesy of the Royal Museums of Scotland

CHARLES MACLAREN

CHARLES MACLAREN, co-founder and originally and for nearly thirty years joint editor and later first editor of *The Scotsman*, resided in "Morelands" in Whitehouse Terrace, which became part of the Astley Ainslie Hospital. While Maclaren paid so much tribute to his great friend and co-founder of *The Scotsman*, William

Charles MacLaren

Ritchie, who resided some distance westwards at "Hebron Bank" in Canaan Lane, the impression might be gained that he himself played a very minor role in what was, at the time, a quite incredibly bold and highly principled undertaking. This would be quite false. Charles Maclaren was distinguished in scientific circles and was elected a Fellow of the Royal Society of Edinburgh and president of the Edinburgh Geological Society. He was of very different temperament from Ritchie and their foundation partnership was most fortuitous for its time.

Charles Maclaren was the son of a small-scale farmer and cattle-dealer and was born at Ormiston in East Lothian on October 7th 1782. Though he received some formal education, he was mainly self-taught. He went to Edinburgh and worked as a clerk and book-keeper, eventually acquiring quite a high post in the Customs and Excise. It was in the Philomathic Debating Society that he first met William Ritchie, duly leading to their joint journalistic enterprise. In their association on *The Scotsman* it was Maclaren who steered the undertaking through difficult and near critical times with characteristic coolness and caution. These were not only financial crises but also the reaction to their policies on parliamentary and municipal reform, Catholic Emancipation, and other very controversial issues. While as a writer Ritchie was "quick, nimble and fluent", his partner was more slow and laborious, although his style was clear and sharp, at times stiff and abrupt. Ritchie would assist Maclaren when he had to write quickly to meet a deadline. They struck an excellent balance. Nevertheless Maclaren could be fearless in his printed commentaries, and on one occasion, smarting under his words, Dr James Browne, Editor of *The Caledonian Mercury*, in the autumn of 1829 challenged him to a duel, no less. At the appointed hour, at Ravelston Road near Bell's Mill, the contestants duly appeared. Dr Browne was seconded by Mr Peterkin and Mr Liston, the noted surgeon, while Maclaren's seconds were a Mr L. MacDonald and the distinguished surgeon and fellow-Canaanite Professor James Syme. Paces were measured, the first shots fired but wide of their respective targets. Eventually, although apparently a little half-hearted, there was hand-shaking all round and the company returned unharmed to the city.

In 1820 Maclaren had edited the sixth edition of the *Encyclopaedia*

Britannica for Archibald Constable, contributing several articles himself. Elected F.R.S.E. in 1837 and a Fellow of the London Geological Society in 1846, it was Maclaren with his deep interest in geology who in 1840 brought his friend, the distinguished Swiss geologist Louis Agassiz, to see the rock near the entrance to the subsequent Blackford Quarry. After studying it Agassiz proclaimed an answer to the controversies which had raged with the words: "This is the work of the ice". The rock bears a plaque commemorating the occasion. Maclaren published much work on geology. In January 1842 he had married Jean Veitch, widow of David Hume, nephew of the famous philosopher.

DAVID AINSLIE OF COSTERTON

David Ainslie of Costerton
By courtesy of Mr R. Copeland
formerly of the Astley Ainslie Hospital

OF those associated with Canaan in more recent times David Ainslie of Costerton in East Lothian is impressively and appreciatively commemorated by the beautifully situated Astley Ainslie Hospital in Canaan Lane. David Ainslie was a seventh-generation descendant of David Ainslie of Fala. He was born on the 4th April 1813 to William Ainslie of Huntingdon and his wife Martha Skirving. It was through the marriage of David Ainslie's brother John to Cordelia Astley that eventually the hospital was to be given its twin names.

The date on which David Ainslie purchased the estate of Costerton near Crichton Castle is not clearly on record, but there in its pleasant pasture lands he became an expert and prosperous sheep breeder and was awarded many trophies for his skill. In his will he directed that these be presented to the Scottish Industrial Museum (now the Royal Museum of Scotland) in Chambers Street or displayed in the hospital which he requested should be built from a substantial bequest from his estate. They are now in a special display cabinet in the Astley Ainslie Hospital.

Ainslie, who was unmarried, originally intended to settle a large part of his estate on his nephew, John Astley Ainslie, an Oxford graduate and barrister, but he died in Algiers in 1874, pre-deceasing his uncle by twenty-six years. David Ainslie therefore directed that the sum of approximately £800,000 be devoted to the purpose "of erecting, endowing and maintaining a hospital or institution for the relief and behoof of the convalescents of the Royal Infirmary of Edinburgh". The hospital envisaged originally was to have been named "St John's Hospital" but Ainslie altered his will to have it named instead "The Astley Ainslie Institution" (later Hospital) in memory of his nephew. He also specified that the building should be "of a Grecian style of architecture to reproduce that of John Watson's Hospital" in Belford Road. This was not implemented, but Ainslie's request that the hospital be built in the Grange district of Edinburgh or nearby was observed by the purchase of 42 acres of land at the east end of Canaan Lane on what was once part of the ancient Burgh Muir and around the site of the long-since demolished old chapel of St Roque, centre of the quarantine area for centuries of the victims of the plague. Several properties with early 19th-century villas were included in the purchase and duly incorporated into the hospital.

David Ainslie died at Costerton on May 24th 1900 and was buried in Crichton parish churchyard. A waiting-period of fifteen years was arranged for his estate to accrue. The First World War intervened meanwhile and the Astley Ainslie Hospital was not built until 1923, and then in stages. While retaining its original function as specified by Ainslie, the hospital over the years has widened its scope to meet changing health service requirements, and several fine new buildings have been added.

Sydney Thompson Dobell
by Briton Rivière
by courtesy of the National Portrait Gallery, London

SYDNEY DOBELL

FREQUENTLY over the years in booklets dealing with some other subject authors have included material on the local history of associated places. Thus, Robert Cochrane in his small book *Pentland Walks*, which is something of a minor classic and though long out of print is still eagerly sought, in referring to the Canaan estate in Morningside *en route* to the Pentlands states: "To one of these cottages came Sydney Dobell, the poet, in search of health and quiet". Often such isolated statements cannot be verified from printed sources but in this instance Cochrane is correct in general as regards Morningside, if not specifically Canaan. In *The Life and Letters of Sydney Dobell*, published in 1878 and edited by "E.J.", and in other biographical works on the English poet, it is related that in 1854 he came to Edinburgh seeking medical advice concerning the condition of his wife, but no indication is given as regards precisely where he then resided. In 1866, however, Dobell had been visiting Naples, and while studying certain ancient ruins there, he stumbled and suffered a quite serious fall. His health was severely impaired. In his *Life and Letters* one

199

passage referring to 1866 states: "A little house was taken at Morningside and in the fresher air he seemed to recover". There is no address given of where he resided and he may well have taken tenancy of a cottage in Canaan as Cochrane states.

Dobell, who was born in Kent in April 1824, came to Scotland at intervals over a period of three years in search of better health, spending the winters in Edinburgh and the summers in the Highlands. While in England he had cultivated friendships with Tennyson, Carlyle, Charlotte Brontë, Ruskin, and Gabriel Rossetti, and in Edinburgh he made the acquaintance of Dr William Hanna, Dr Thomas Chalmers' son-in-law and biographer, Sir David Brewster, Miss Catherine Sinclair, Dr John Brown, Professor James Y. Simpson and Professor Piazzi Smyth, the astronomer. Dobell died in August 1875.

James Wilson

From: "Memoirs of the Life of James Wilson, Esq., of Woodville" by James Hamilton

JAMES WILSON

WHEN in the early 19th century a writer described those who had come out from the city to reside in the villas of Canaan, he referred to them as "ensconced in their snug boxes". To none would these words apply more aptly than to "Woodville", hidden away behind its high walls at the north-west corner of Canaan Lane and Newbattle Terrace. When James Wilson shortly after his marriage in 1824 took up residence in "Woodville" his biographer was later to write that there "he caught the whole sunshine of the winter noon forgetful of biting blasts and easterly fogs".

Not only did "Woodville" enjoy such a fine climatic setting but its windows looked southwards over a most extensive lawn and garden enclosed by fine trees towards the Pentland Hills, and it was a garden of unique interest in terms of plants and wildlife. Despite such an idyllic setting, James Wilson himself was perhaps mostly too occupied with his writing, except when he lifted his head from his desk, to notice his surroundings. Brother of the better known John Wilson, "Christopher North", Wilson was nevertheless a naturalist of world-wide repute and never tired of telling of the letter which was simply addressed:

Mr Wilson
Lover of Insects,
Morningside,
Edinburgh

which reached him safely! Wilson was joint author with his great friend and not too distant neighbour, Sir Thomas Dick Lauder of the Grange House, of *Voyage Round the Coasts of Scotland*, author of *Illustrations of Zoology* in nine quarto volumes; also of all the material for the Natural History section of the 7th edition of the *Encyclopaedia Britannica*. In 1854 he declined the Chair of Natural History at Edinburgh University, largely on health grounds. He died at "Woodville" in 1856.

After Wilson's death his niece Henrietta Wilson came to live at "Woodville" and spent a great deal of her time in the garden. She left a fascinating record in *Chronicles of a Garden: Its Pets and Pleasures*, published in 1864. At the present time of writing, and in view of the building which is now taking place in several of the hitherto large open spaces and gardens of Canaan, a source of some concern to many Morningside residents, Miss Wilson's book, which is now found only in rare collections, has come to attract renewed attention for the picture it gives of the natural and cultivated attractions of the district a century and more ago and now, it is feared, about to steadily disappear for ever. Strangely, in her own day, Miss Wilson was equally concerned about the felling of trees in Canaan to make way for additional villas. She herself, as she records, could not bear to remove daisies from the lawn or destroy the more attractive weeds! A remarkable lady, her whole life, however, was not given over to "Woodville" and its garden. She spent much time working among the lonely and neglected sick of the Cowgate and indeed she wrote *Pleasures of a Garden* to raise funds on behalf of the Medical Missionary Sick Visiting Fund whose members worked in the slums. Sadly, she died before the book was published.

THOMAS CAMPBELL

Thomas Campbell
by Sir Thomas Laurence
By courtesy of the National Galleries of Scotland, Edinburgh

IN the annals of "Woodville" we encounter another poet. In Dr W. Beattie's *Life and Letters of Thomas Campbell*, there are many references to the famous Scottish poet's visit to Edinburgh and in particular to "Woodville", in the 1830s, which he enjoyed greatly, visiting the Reverend Archibald Alison, Rector of the Episcopalian chapel in the Cowgate, which subsequently became St Patrick's Roman Catholic Church, and was later Rector of St Paul's in York Place. During a visit to "Woodville" in August 1837 Campbell planted a tree in the garden but this has not survived. Born in

201

Glasgow in 1777, of a family whose origins were in Inveraray on Loch Fyne, Campbell is best known perhaps for his *Ye Mariners of England* and *Pleasures of Hope*. He received much valuable public notice from Professor Gregory of Canaan Lodge, adjacent to "Woodville", and some of his work was illustrated by Turner in engravings by William Miller of Millerfield Place beside the Meadows.

SIR JAMES RUSSELL

Lord Provost Sir James Russell

Reproduced from "The Lord Provosts of Edinburgh"
By courtesy of the City of Edinburgh Art Centre

AFTER the deaths of James Wilson and his wife, of "Woodville", and of Wilson's niece Henrietta, the secluded villa became the quiet retreat of another very busy professional man, Sir James Russell, who had married one of Wilson's daughters. Russell, son of the Free Church minister at Colintraive in the Kyles of Bute, graduated in medicine in Edinburgh University and specialised in Public Health, one of the early pioneers in this relatively new sphere. He became a Town Councillor in 1877 and Lord Provost in 1891. James Russell played an important part in the city's public health development and was much involved in the completion of the City Fever Hospital in Greenbank Drive in 1903. He also assisted in planning the new North Bridge, was awarded an LL.D. by the University and died on January 22nd 1918.

CANON JOHN GRAY and ANDRE RAFFALOVITCH

AMONG the few notable former "residenters" of South Edinburgh in whom, after a considerable passage of time, a significant and continuing interest remains to stimulate further research and re-assessment, are Canon John Gray and his close friend André Raffalovitch. If a number of those distinguished in the world of literature may still be seen passing along Whitehouse Terrace, they are likely to be in Edinburgh either to attend the International Festival Book Fair or perhaps a "Meet the Authors" session, and not now (as at the turn of the century) as guests of André Raffalovitch at one of his Tuesday literary lunches or Sunday dinner parties, when his house at No 9 was something of a writers' and artists' Mecca.

Interest has remained and indeed deepened and widened in Gray and Raffalovitch, primarily, if not almost

Canon John Gray

From drawing by Austin Osman Spare, c.1910
In a private collection

become a close friend of his hero Oscar Wilde. There followed his own excursions into poetry, impressing critics at the time and now attracting renewed favourable attention. Raffalovitch was a member of a wealthy exiled Russian Jewish family in Paris. His mother's fashionable literary salon introduced him to the leading French writers and in turn to the equivalent London scene and his friendship with John Gray, ending only with their deaths in Edinburgh.

In the text of *In the Dorian Mode* Father Sewell examines the Oscar Wilde-John Gray relationship and all its implications, including the court action and the end of their friendship. He reviews, too, John Gray's departure for the Scots College in Rome to study for the Catholic priesthood, his first curacy at St Patrick's in the Cowgate, with

exclusively, through the publication by their principal biographer, Father Brocard Sewell, of the early *Two Friends* and *Footnote to the Nineties* and most recently the first proper biography of Canon Gray: *In the Dorian Mode*. A symposium on the two very dissimilar yet close friends, held in 1984 and organised by Mr Gordon Campbell, attended by Father Sewell and several people who had known both Gray and Raffalovitch, was very well attended, and produced much new material. Here in Father Sewell's latest long-researched and scholarly study the paths of the two men before they met are traced. Gray, from a large working-class family in London, was reluctantly forced to leave school at the age of 14 to supplement the family income. He continued to study at night-classes and eventually qualified to become in 1888 a Foreign Office librarian, thus John Gray was enabled to move in the London theatre "first-night" world of writers, poets, the intellectually "smart set", and in such circles to

André Raffalovich

From a painting by A. Dampier May, 1886
In a private collection

203

the former dandified poet now fearlessly going on sick calls, moving amongst the forbidding closes and tenements of a locality in which even the police did not relish their duties. He tells of the resumption of the intellectual, cultivated life-style as John Gray becomes parish priest of the specially built St Peter's Church in Falcon Avenue in 1906, a masterpiece by Sir Robert Lorimer, leading architect of his day, the cost largely borne by Raffalovitch, to be near which Raffalovitch purchased the fine villa at 9 Whitehouse Terrace. Here "anyone who was anybody" in the literary world, visiting Edinburgh or invited, being the guests of the impeccable hosts, Raffalovitch and his housekeeper, recreated something of the intellectual atmosphere of the early days of "The Two Friends" in London. "The mysterious and fascinating" and lengthy story was to come to an end, after nearly thirty years, quite suddenly. André Raffalovitch, who attended St Peter's daily for Communion, was found dead on the morning of February 14th 1934. The Requiem Mass and the funeral to Mount Vernon Cemetery were conducted by Canon Gray. It was a bitterly cold day and the priest, attired in thin surplice and vestments, caught a chill, developed pneumonia and, his health having deteriorated, died four months later. It was the end of a story of which, it would appear, more may still remain to be told.

3 · BEYOND THE JORDAN

FOR centuries the Pow or Jordan Burn was Edinburgh's southern boundary; it ran from the lower slopes of Easter Craiglockhart Hill, or Craighouse Hill, by the side of the old suburban railway line, under Morningside Road near Braid Church and Morningside Post Office, onwards and eastwards by the Astley Ainslie Hospital, under Blackford Avenue, Mayfield Road eventually to Peffermill and its union with the larger Braid Burn. Thus, in early times, by crossing the wooden bridge over the Jordan at the Briggs o' Braid beside the old toll-house at the foot of Morningside Road, so colourfully described by Robert Louis Stevenson in his *Edinburgh: Picturesque Notes**, one was leaving Edinburgh and passing into pathways through open fields to Blackford, Braid, Plewlands, Greenbank and Comiston to Swanston. Edinburgh's southern boundary now runs along the top ridge of Caerketton above the artificial ski slope; but to cross the Jordan still recalls leaving the old village of Morningside and entering the quite different districts beyond. In presenting interesting people who have resided in or been associated with South Edinburgh the Jordan forms a historically significant dividing line. As we cross it two people come to mind immediately who certainly merit consideration.

*Republished as *Picturesque Old Edinburgh*, Charles Skilton, 1984.

SIR GEORGE WASHINGTON BROWNE

Sir George Washington Browne
by A. E. Borthwick
By courtesy of the National Galleries of Scotland, Edinburgh

WHEN in the passage referred to above in his *Edinburgh: Picturesque Notes*, published in 1878, Stevenson described the chisels tinkling just beyond the old toll-house, he may have been referring to the building of Maxwell Street or the earliest houses in Nile Grove. Not long afterwards, however, in 1886, the chisels began tinkling on the building of Braid Church at the north-west corner of Nile Grove, and tinkling under the direction of one of Edinburgh's most eminent architects of the late 19th century, George Washington Browne. Compared with Browne's much better known work in the city,

205

such as the Central Public Library at George IV Bridge, (1890), The Royal Hospital for Sick Children in Sciennes Road (1895), the King Edward VII memorial at Holyrood Palace, or his extension to the Advocate's Library, Braid Church may seem a very minor work, yet it was of some architectural interest, stemming from the consultation between George Washington Browne and Braid Church's first minister, the Reverend Walter Brown, when it was agreed that instead of a more traditional style of church building the architect would build "an auditorium, enabling a semi-circle of people to gather eagerly round a speaker".

George Washington Browne was born in Glasgow in 1853 and received his early training there, followed by a short period in London. There he gained several prizes, including a Pugin Studentship — the first Scotsman to win this much coveted prize. In 1879 he returned to Edinburgh to become chief assistant to the eminent Sir Rowand Anderson, an appointment of some achievement and prestige. During five very busy years with Sir Rowand he assisted in the building of the McEwan Hall, which reveals several Washington Browne features. In 1886 the famous philanthropist Andrew Carnegie wrote to Edinburgh's Lord Provost, Sir Thomas Clark, praising Edinburgh as a city and offering to add his contribution to its many attractions in the form of a "free library" — if the citizens were "of the opinion that this would be of practical good to the city". Carnegie offered £25,000. A few days later, in a cable, he doubled his offer. At two earlier public meetings proposals of a central rate-supported "free library" were rejected. At a further public gathering of 2,000 people Carnegie's generous offer was reported, and the building of a city library was agreed. While Andrew Carnegie's offer of £50,000 was sent to and accepted by Lord Provost Thomas Clark, it was apparently the wealthy benefactor's close friendship with Sir Thomas's predecessor in office, Sir George Harrison, which led to his substantial gift to the city.

After the choice of George IV Bridge as the appropriate site, and official deputations had visited English cities, along with Edinburgh's City Architect Mr Robert Morham, to study libraries in the south, designs for the new Edinburgh library were invited. Of the 32 plans submitted at first none was considered suitable, but eventually George Washington Browne was awarded a £100 premium and the commission to build. His design was of French Renaissance style. The George IV Bridge library was formally opened by Lord Rosebery on June 9th 1890. Washington Browne's creation of the new library firmly established his private business, and many important contracts followed, some of these in London. The spacious high quality flats at Bruntsfield between Forbes Road and Bruntsfield Gardens were, in fact, a replica of a row he built in London.

George Washington Browne was President of the Edinburgh Architectural Association 1884-86. In 1924 he was elected President of the Royal Scottish Academy — the first architect to hold this office, which he did for ten years. Browne was a traditionalist in his approach and critical of "originality which had no origin". He was awarded an LL.D. by Edinburgh University and received a knighthood in 1926. At 35 Blackford Road stands the very fine house which Browne built as a gift for his first wife, Jessie Brownlie, whom he married in 1881, but who died before its completion in 1899. He remarried, and many years later moved to Randolph Cliff, where he died in 1939. His three sons were killed in the Second World War, and he was survived by a married daughter. Several of the personal reminiscences of George Washington Browne's friends stress his imposing air of dignity and his courtly manner and a distinctive personality that lives vividly in the memory. Away from the drawing board he enjoyed nothing better than a game of billiards!

Sir Thomas Bouch

By courtesy of the National Library of Scotland, Edinburgh

SIR THOMAS BOUCH

ROBERT LOUIS STEVENSON reacted indignantly to the building of "the new row of houses beyond the toll", which he was sure would spoil the green meadows beyond the Jordan; one can but conjecture what his reactions might have been to the opening some years later of the suburban railway which, by its almost revolutionary opening up of transport facilities to and from the city, was to lead to Morningside's mushroom growth almost overnight and especially of the "villadom" which R.L.S. foresaw arising in the Cluny, Braid Road area. The person responsible for this new development destined to change the face of Morningside, and other districts, was a man "awaiting sentence" for his possible culpability in the tragedy of the Tay Bridge disaster on December 28th 1879. This man was Sir Thomas Bouch, who resided in Comely Bank.

Thomas Bouch was born in Thursley in Cumberland on February 22nd 1822, the third son of a captain in the Mercantile Marine. In boyhood he was fascinated by mechanics, and at the age of 17 began an apprenticeship in mechanical engineering. After acquiring some experience he was soon proposing "floating railways" across various rivers including the Forth and Tay. He designed many railway systems as well as tramway tracks, in the North of England and some in Edinburgh. But his most ambitious creation was the Tay Bridge, completed and opened in 1878. Bouch was presented with the freedom of Dundee and in 1879 was knighted. Only a few months later disaster struck. On the night of Sunday, December 28th 1879, during a violent gale, the central portion of the bridge collapsed and a train which was crossing plunged into the water below. All seventy passengers were drowned.

A Board of Trade Court of Inquiry was opened in Dundee; the proceedings lasted from January until May 1880. While obviously affected in his health by this disaster, Bouch nevertheless protested his blamelessness, and with confidence undertook — and perhaps rather surprisingly was given — other public work. This included the planning of the Edinburgh Suburban and South Side Junction Railway. The project required parliamentary sanction and Bouch travelled frequently to London to provide details and for consultations. His diary for August 6th 1880 read: "Suburban Railway before committee. Preamble approved. Travelled to Edinbro". On arrival back in Edinburgh Bouch felt unwell and his doctor ordered him to have complete rest, which he sought at Moffat. There he died in October 1880. Bouch's Suburban Railway plans eventually received parliamentary approval, but Bouch had been dead for four years when the first trains ran in December 1884. For long the suburban system was highly successful, with a train service into and out of Waverley Station round the circular route every ten minutes at the peak hours. Greatly increased use of motor cars, an improved bus service, and other factors, led to the closing of the suburban railway in 1962. At the time of writing, however, there are signs of consider-able interest among South Edinburgh residents in the possible re-opening of the railway system, and several "re-runs" have attracted a substantial response.

SUBURBAN TRAVELLERS

THE opening of the Suburban Railway in 1884 made travel to and from the city very much more convenient, not to say quicker, than by horse-drawn transport, thus leading virtually overnight, so to speak, to the mushroom growth of Morningside as a desirable residential area. The new travel facilities and the railway freight yard at the end of Maxwell Street also facilitated the bulk delivery of commodities for the many and varied shops which were opened in Morningside Road and Comiston Road. The railway also made the journey to Morningside much easier for a certain lady who travelled out to the growing suburb daily from Fisherrow. She was a fishwife named Bella Gibson, who made her way from Morningside Station with a heavy creel on her back and attired in the colourful costume of the Firth of Forth fishwives, to the newly-built villas of Cluny and Midmar. In doing so she was succeeding her mother in pioneering the establishment at the turn of the century of what still remains Morningside's longest-established family business — that of Robert Main, fishmonger.

An Edinburgh writer of the mid-19th century had remarked that even at that time the city was expanding steadily to the south, with an increasing number of people taking up residence there in the new, and

Kirsty Barrie
Early Fishwife

By courtesy of Mr Gilmour Main

then still quite remote, villas in their pleasant rural setting. Writing of this new era he commented somewhat poetically: "Now the cry of the fishwife is heard in Canaan": who this earliest fishwife was is not on record but certainly soon after this period we do know that Canaan would have echoed to the cry of Bella Gibson's mother, Kirsty Barrie, a Fisherrow fishwife possibly with a Dutch family background. Her usual cry might have been the traditional "Caller herrin'!'": on certain days, though, it would have proclaimed that oysters were also for sale. These delicacies were carried by Bella, Kirsty's young daughter, then in her early teens. Bella's son, octogenarian Gilmour Main, who still does his daily stint of service in the family shop, relates that apparently his mother found the door-to-door selling a long, long

walk and would wearily inquire of his grandmother: "How much further is there to go?" Thus while in her day Kirsty Barrie's journey from Fisherrow to the important busy Newhaven fishmarket would have been by cart and then eventually by horse-drawn bus to Morningside, her daughter Bella in later years enjoyed the convenience and speedier pace of the Suburban Railway. Eventually, at the turn of the century, Bella Gibson was able to find relief from her long walks round the Morningside villas when with her husband Robert Main they opened their first fishmonger's shop in Morningside Road.

In the days before the prevalence of the motor-car the Edinburgh Suburban Railway proved invaluable to Morningside's numerous commuters, and their counterparts in other city suburbs, many in conventional businessmen's attire and with brief-case and rolled umbrella, travelling to and from Waverley and Haymarket stations and thence to their offices in the city. At the peak periods trains ran every ten minutes and were very well

Commuters on former Suburban Railway arriving at Morningside Road Station

*Torrance – Morningside's early established bakers at corner of Comiston Road
and Belhaven Terrace*

patronised. So too the "football specials" on Saturdays conveying faithful supporters of the Heart of Midlothian and Hibernian football teams. Finally, and as a social commentary on the thirties' era of depression, the early morning suburban trains around 6 a.m. brought very many adults and numbers of quite young children from the poorer parts of the city, who alighted at Morningside and, equipped with large pillow-cases, literally raced to the local bakers' shops to purchase "old teabread" at much reduced price.

4 · BLACKFORD

MENIE TROTTER

INNUMERABLE people residing in the Morningside area, although not knowing who she was or any other details, seem to have heard of the old lady who lived in Blackford House and who bathed daily in the Jordan Burn which flowed through her garden. The lady was, of course, Miss Menie Trotter, and since the publication of my earlier volume more information concerning "the lady of Blackford", and indeed about the house itself, has come to light. For this I am greatly indebted to a Morningside lady who was related to Miss Trotter's much-esteemed maidservant and companion, Mrs Peggie Douglas, and who donated to the National Library of Scotland two lengthy and interesting letters of Miss Trotter's, which had long been in her possession. These were letters written to her maid after the latter had left her service and returned full-time to her home at Edgehead, near Ford, where her husband Robert Douglas was a smith and a farrier. Furthermore, the Morningside lady has in her possession an original painting of Blackford House by an itinerant artist, showing Miss Trotter in her much younger days, and this she kindly allowed me to copy for reproduction here.

One valuable feature of the two letters, apart from their interesting content, was that they were dated, one for March 1st 1835, and the other for July 11th 1835. Previously dates relating to Miss Trotter's occupancy

Miss Menie Trotter at Blackford House, her dog on her left and a friend holding rake on her right while her servant is using watering can
Artist unknown
By courtesy of Mrs H. Meikle

of Blackford House have been somewhat imprecise. Those appearing on the letters facilitated further research into various library archives and brought to light a lengthy article in *The Scotsman* of March 5th 1938 by Mr W. Forbes Gray, an authority on the history of South Edinburgh, dealing primarily with Blackford House then still extant (although standing empty and with an uncertain future), but also providing much interesting information about Miss Trotter herself. Other printed sources dealing with the early 19th-century Edinburgh lady novelist of East Morningside House, Susan Ferrier, also provided further insight concerning Miss Trotter. Miss Ferrier's father, Mr James Ferrier, was Miss Trotter's lawyer and indeed Susan got to know the old lady quite well and may have introduced her as a character into some of her novels.

The two letters addressed to Mrs Peggie Douglas give a wealth of detail concerning Miss Trotter's "daily round" at Blackford; her small farm with its "little cow" which was not being very skilfully handled by a new servant; her purchase of marmalade oranges; the awaiting of the chimney sweep; a friend going to a new post on some Mediterranean island at an unusually high salary; and another friend, having developed "the fidgets", going to London. She also mentions the various ladies who were her friends, with whom she corresponded or who visited her, such as Mrs Grant of Laggan. The latter, always impressed by Miss Trotter's generous hospitality and her "open house" for fashionable and literary ladies, wrote to Mrs Fletcher at Auchendinny House (and who was once a tenant of Egypt Farm) extolling the virtues of the Blackford hostess.

The old newspaper articles also indicate that Miss Trotter was born in the middle of the 18th century, daughter of Thomas Trotter, 7th Laird of Mortonhall, who died in 1793, leaving three sons and six daughters. Miss Menie chose to live at Blackford House, a Trotter dower house. The house was early 18th-century, of little architectural interest. Its main entrance faced east. Its grounds had been more extensive in Miss Trotter's day but part of them were sold when the suburban railway track and station were being laid out at Blackford Hill in the early 1880s, cutting off the main entrance avenue and original pillared gateway. Sir Thomas Dick Lauder, her near neighbour at Grange House, in his book *Scottish Rivers*, drawn from his personal recollections, confirmed the accounts of her early morning bathing sessions in the Jordan Burn and that she would afterwards walk over Blackford Hill before breakfast.

Miss Trotter, who had an innate trust in people's honesty, especially of her servants, kept two large jars on her dressing-table, one holding silver coins, the other coppers. Once she sent a £50 note wrapped in a cabbage leaf, by a servant to a friend across the city. She completely distrusted banks and kept her bank-notes and accounts in a green silk bag which hung from her wall mirror. She was a lady of great generosity. Upon hearing of the premature death of the parents of a large family she knew, she immediately sent £2,000 to support the orphaned children. She stood surety for £500 for a boy convicted of theft and found him a job in London, where he later achieved considerable success. Miss Trotter, even in advanced age, did not remain house-bound at Black-Blackford. In her social round she was a frequent guest of the distinguished Professor William Cullen of the Edinburgh Medical School, whose home was renowned for its hospitality and interesting visitors. Towards the end of her life she often remarked to close friends that although she had never married she had once been the "sweetheart of Dr James Pitcairn", but her parents had disapproved of her marrying him. Neither she nor "Dr Jamie" had ever wed. Miss Trotter died in about 1840, aged nearly 100. She was buried in the Trotter family mausoleum at Mortonhall House.

Lord Provost Sir George Harrison with Blackford Plan

by William Hole
From "Quasi Cursores", Portraits of the High Officers and Professors of the University of Edinburgh at its Tercentenary, 1884

LORD PROVOST SIR GEORGE HARRISON

OF Edinburgh's 800-plus "presentation seats" (their official name) it is believed that the distinction of occupying the highest vantage point could be claimed by that installed in 1984 on the lofty 500-foot summit of Blackford Hill. Though the inscription is brief: "Presented by the family in memory of Sir George Harrison, M.P., LL.D.", there was certainly nothing brief about the distinguished record of one of the city's most public-spirited Lord Provosts. It is the successful outcome of one of his many campaigns which the seat commemorates: his acquisition for the city in the spring of 1884, of Blackford Hill and its very pleasant amenities.

When nearly a century earlier young Walter Scott was inspired to wax poetic over the magnificent panorama he enjoyed when as "a truant boy" he gazed down upon "mine own romantic town", his "truancy" may have been unauthorised absence from school or trespassing upon what was then the private property of the famous Trotters of Mortonhall. Or perhaps they had granted him this privilege to roam happily amongst the Blackford's "broom and thorn and whin". Scott's private privilege it might have been, but Lord Provost Harrison, frustrated in his own attempts to walk freely in his precious leisure time upon the Blackford slopes, was determined that access should become every citizen's right. His campaign did not receive unqualified support. City Treasurer Boyd was strongly opposed, arguing that the £800 purchase price demanded "was not a bargain", and that Edinburgh's

213

citizens should simply pay the £1 entrance fee and "not seek their pleasures on the rates". Furthermore, he insisted, "Blackford Hill is quite unsuitable for football, golf and cricket". However, as the Town Council minutes reveal, Sir George Harrison won the day, surely earning the gratitude of countless citizens and visitors over the century since. Harrison Park on the west side of the city commemorates this much respected Lord Provost but Blackford Hill might equally have been so named, as the great memorial arch at the entrance to Observatory Road proclaims.

The acquisition of Blackford was but one of Sir George Harrison's almost innumerable commitments, the catalogue of which reads like a directory of public bodies. He was a native of Stonehaven, and after successfully establishing a clothier's business in Edinburgh his public service began: Secretary, then Chairman of the Chamber of Commerce, Liberal Town Councillor for Newington, and Lord Provost from 1882 to 1885. He was much involved in the restoration of St Giles Cathedral and the staging of Scotland's first forestry exhibition; and became a director of the North British Railway Company, the Edinburgh Gas Council and the Water Trust, serving on government commissions for educational and legal reforms, the housing of "the working class", and the nationalisation of the telegraph service. Yet he still found time to co-found the Philosophical Institute and to form an Edinburgh branch of "the Friends of Italy", personally enlisting moral and financial support for Garibaldi who had the Freedom of the City of Edinburgh conferred upon him (*in absentia*) in 1864. Garibaldi's personal letter of appreciation to Sir George Harrison is now a treasured family archive.

A close friend of Andrew Carnegie, Sir George had much influence as regards the wealthy benefactor's gift to the city of the Central Public Library building in George IV Bridge, designed by the notable architect George Washington Browne, another close friend. Sir George Harrison officiated at the opening of the new Medical School in Teviot Place in 1884 and was awarded a knighthood the same year. He was elected MP for South Edinburgh in 1885 but he died soon after going to Westminster. The tradition of public service continued in the Harrison family, who resided in Sir James Gowans' "architecturally astonishing" house, "Rockville" in Napier Road (known as the "Pagoda House") for fifty years. Sir George's son John became City Treasurer, his daughter Agnes a senior baillie. When in her nineties she was still actively interested in social questions. His other daughter Nell purchased Gladstone's Land in the Lawnmarket and donated it to the National Trust. Grandson Alexander ("Sandy") Harrison, a former Town Councillor and prominent in Edinburgh public life, while himself a nonagenarian, organised the installation of the Blackford Hill seat.

LOUIS AGASSIZ

"In 1840, Charles Maclaren showed this scratched and polished stone to Agassiz who exclaimed: 'This is the work of the ice'."

214

Louis Agassiz
Engraving from photograph by C. H. Jeens
From "Louis Agassiz: His Life & Correspondence". Ed. by
Elizabeth Cary Agassiz

A BRIEF and apparently simple and inconsequential statement it may well appear to the layman, but these words on the metal plaque placed in front of the great rock at the foot of the hillside at Blackford Glen on the north bank of the Braid Burn near the now disused quarry reverberated within the world of geologists as loudly as any detonation that ever echoed from Blackford Quarry. To those interested, or indeed expert in the science of geology, the dictum so confidently and dramatically uttered by the world-famous Swiss geologist, Louis Agassiz, as he completed his examination of the rock here in 1840 itself stilled a controversy that had continued to rage in various parts of the world concerning the effects and the evidence left behind by melting glaciers as the Ice Age ended and the massive glacial formations slowly slid downwards. During their passage their weight and shape cleft great gorges and valleys. Nowadays it is known that this is how in remote ages the Braidburn Valley was formed and also the steep and narrow gorge of the Hermitage of Braid and the gentler valley between Blackford Hill and Braid Hills Drive.

But in the early 1800s such action by glaciers and certain aspects of evidence of their existence in various places was not readily or generally accepted. The man who became the world authority on the subject and who solved many of the perennial controversies was Louis Agassiz. The Braidburn Valley and Hermitage route were a case in point. There had been much debate between Edinburgh geologists and Charles Maclaren, co-founder of *The Scotsman* and for nearly thirty years joint editor, then editor, of that famous newspaper. Maclaren was President of the Edinburgh Geological Society from 1864 until his death two years later. He also published *A Sketch of*

The Agassiz Rock
Blackford Glen, Edinburgh
By Courtesy of British Geological Survey

215

the Geology of Fife and the Lothians in 1839. He it was who during one of Agassiz's visits to Scotland persuaded him to examine the rock in Blackford Glen. Even after the apparently decisive statement quoted above various geologists still questioned the Swiss expert's opinion, as they did concerning his observations on other parts of Europe, and the debate indeed continued. However, in relatively recent times, research by Professor Gordon Davies of Trinity College, Dublin, confirmed that Agassiz was correct.

Jean Louis Rodolfe Agassiz was born on May 28th 1807 in the small village of Motier on the Lake of Morat, a continuation of the beautiful Lake Neuchâtel in Switzerland. His father was a clergyman with a very modest stipend and his mother the daughter of a doctor. The parsonage in which he was brought up was very picturesquely situated on the lakeside facing the Bernese Alps. From an early age young Louis showed signs of becoming the dedicated scholar he was to prove to be, not only the author of many books and an eagerly sought lecturer, but leader of very many daring and dangerous expeditions and exploits in the European Alps. He undertook such quests in Britain also and eventually in numerous parts of North and South America. From early childhood Agassiz showed a keen interest in natural history, collecting specimens of insects, flowers and small animals.

After attending a boys' college at Bienne, instead of entering upon the traditional apprenticeship in some small business, Agassiz pleaded with his parents to permit him two years' further study at Lausanne. They readily agreed, though at considerable financial sacrifice, which tended to create feelings of concern and guilt in young Louis for many years. Next, now rather against his own interests but to please his parents, who saw no secure future for him in the further study of natural history, he began the study of medicine at Zürich, continuing at Heidelberg in 1826. Many letters he wrote to his father reveal his lack of interest in medicine but both his parents insisted that at least he should obtain his medical degree and have the security of this profession to fall back upon before taking up a career in natural history. Agassiz acquiesced and duly obtained his doctorate in medicine at Munich in 1830, aged 24, to add to a diploma he had already gained in natural history.

His university studies over, Agassiz lost no time in pursuing his primary scientific interests, and he found that a book he had published in 1829 on a study of Brazilian fish had created quite a profound impression. In 1832 he accepted the Chair in Natural History at Neuchâtel. His reputation as a scholar and research worker soon spread, and he was awarded a special prize by the Geological Society of London. In 1834 he paid his first visit to England and to Edinburgh. A few years later he published much new material on glaciers and in 1840 he addressed a meeting of the British Association in Glasgow, and after touring the Highlands to observe the effects of the glaciers on the mountains there, his findings corresponding with those already noted in the Alps, he visited Edinburgh and with Charles Maclaren and others visited the rock which bears his name in Blackford Glen. While in Edinburgh Agassiz addressed its Geological Society, and he may also have met Hugh Miller, with whom he had frequently corresponded. In 1841 Professor James D. Forbes, of Edinburgh University, son of Sir William Forbes of Pitsligo and Greenhill, and subsequently Principal of St Andrews University, along with other British scientists, visited Agassiz in Switzerland and accompanied him on glacier study expeditions, often involving considerable danger, especially on the Jungfrau, under the entirely fearless leadership of the famous Swiss geologist.

In September 1846 Louis Agassiz sailed for the United States of America and landed at Boston. His lectures and observations on glacial phenomena in North and South America were eagerly awaited. He made innumerable, exhaustive and exhausting expeditions to the principal mountain ranges and major cities of this vast continent. In April 1848 he accepted the Chair of Natural History at a college associated with Harvard University and eventually made his home in Cambridge, Massachussets, where he died on December 14th 1873. He was buried at Mount Auburn, and the large boulder which constituted his monument was brought from his beloved glacier at Aar in Switzerland, scene of his early researches and of his famous mountain "hotel" or refuge. Pine trees from Switzerland also surround his grave.

PROFESSOR CHARLES PIAZZI SMYTH

THE Royal Observatory on Blackford Hill is a prominent landmark on Edinburgh's southern skyline. It also constitutes a significant landmark in the development of astronomy in Edinburgh, and indeed the whole of Scotland. Behind its official opening in April 1896 lay much thought and planning and especially the generous patronage in terms of financial support and valuable equipment from Lord Lindsay, the 26th Earl of Crawford and Balcarres, himself an astronomer of distinction. He owned a private observatory at his home in Dunrecht, twelve miles west of Aberdeen, containing first-class instruments of various kinds. During a critical period for the future of astronomy in Edinburgh the Earl of Crawford decided to present to the nation as a gift, not only the instruments in his own observatory, but also his unique astronomy library of 15,000 books, pamphlets and manuscripts, on condition that the Government built and maintained a new Royal Observatory to replace the virtually obsolete one on Calton Hill. This most valuable offer was accepted, and a committee was formed, with the Earl presiding, to choose a site and prepare building plans. In due course the new Royal Observatory at Blackford Hill was opened and in July 1889 Professor Ralph Copland, the Earl of Crawford's own Director of Astronomy at Dunrecht, was appointed 4th Regius Professor of Astronomy at Edinburgh University and 3rd Astronomer-Royal for Scotland.

The establishment of the fine new Observatory ar Blackford Hill at a cost of £30,000 was in many ways a triumph for one man, Charles Piazzi Smyth, Professor of Astronomy in the University and Astronomer-Royal for 42 years, until 1888. Working in the previous observatory on Calton

Professor Piazzi Smyth
by courtesy of the Royal Society of Edinburgh

was given his name, and he expressed the hope that one day the child would also become an astronomer. He fulfilled this hope — with great distinction; he lived to see the new Observatory opened on Blackford Hill and died a few years later, on February 21st 1900. No doubt he gave good reason to be remembered by the people of Edinburgh and countless tourists — even though he may also have caused many of them quite a shock, for he it was who introduced the custom of firing the famous "One o'clock gun" from the Castle. The first inaugural shot was fired on June 5th 1861. The provision of a public service had been required by the government authorities from the Calton Hill Observatory around 1850. The time-ball, hoisted to the top of the Nelson Monument just a short time before one o'clock, dropped when the gun was fired. The dropping of the ball was originally a signal to ships on the Forth. All these arrangements were controlled by a special clock at the Calton Hill Observatory. Later the Observatory controlled similar time-guns at Glasgow and Newcastle-upon-Tyne. For many years the Observatory has no longer been involved in the firing of the Castle gun, which is now controlled entirely by the military authorities, who check their time from the telephonic "speaking clock". The ball is still raised and dropped on the Nelson Monument (now one of Edinburgh District Council's museums), but it is operated manually by a man from an Edinburgh clock-making firm who levers it into position at a few minutes to one o'clock and, watching closely for the puff of smoke from the Castle gun, allows the ball to drop. It is now

Hill he had struggled against serious obstacles in regard to facilities and financial support and had reported to a board of inspectors at Calton Hill that "there are generally no students at all for so untoward, despised and poverty-stricken a subject in Scotland", and that the situation of the Royal Observatory was now "in a ripe state for thorough and searching legislative reform". It was therefore to a large extent the highlighting by Professor Piazzi Smyth of the pitiful state of astronomy in Scotland that brought about the new era — i.e. the Earl of Crawford's generous support and eventually the Government's more serious attention.

Professor Piazzi Smyth was born in Naples on January 3rd 1819, second son of Admiral William Henry Smyth who had become a close friend of the Italian astronomer Giuseppe Piazzi of Palermo. Piazzi acted as godfather to the infant Charles, who unlikely to be watched from Forth-based ships possessing radio communication equipment — unless ship and crew were caught in a "time-warp" and really belong in a bygone age!

5 · BRAID/BUCKSTANE

CHARLES GORDON OF CLUNY

THE earliest, and indeed ancient, lairds of the lands of Braid have been described in an earlier volume, and seem to emerge from antiquity shrouded in a mist of intermingled legend and history. More precise information is on record concerning the acquisition of Braid by a relatively modern owner, Charles Gordon of Cluny, whose other lands in Aberdeenshire ultimately gave rise to many of the present-day street names in the vicinity of the Hermitage of Braid. Unfortunately, not a great deal of detail could be discovered as regards Gordon himself.

Tracing Gordon's ancestry a little into the past, the records refer to a certain John Gordon, born in about 1695, of Glenlivet and Strathaven, factor to the 3rd Duke of Gordon, and who, it would appear, falsely claimed descent from this titled Gordon family. In May 1740 John Gordon is listed as "a merchant in Edinburgh". He had the reputation of being a miser, something of a family trait. Gordon acquired the lands of Cluny in Aberdeenshire in about 1729; he died forty years later. He had three sons, and the eldest, Cosmo, inherited his estate in 1770. He was for some time Rector of Marischal College in Aberdeen and was called to the Scottish Bar in July 1758. Cosmo Gordon died in 1800 without any family and his estate passed in 1805 to his younger brother, Charles, who had already acquired the Braid estate

in 1771. He assumed the title Charles Gordon III of Cluny and I of Braid.

Charles Gordon, whose Edinburgh town-house was at 4 St Andrew Square, had become a Writer to the Signet in 1763 and a Clerk of Session in 1788. In 1772, a year after acquiring Braid, Charles Gordon commissioned for himself a drawing by John Horne of "A Plan of the Barony of Braid: with the Hermitage and Policies, the Property of Charles Gordon Esq.". This is a most interesting and valuable document which gives details not only of the immediate vicinity of the Hermitage of Braid, but also of the Braid Hills and (of special interest to many) the location and extent of Egypt Farm on the northern boundary of the Braid estate at the Jordan Burn, in the area of what is Nile Grove and Woodburn Terrace. On November 8th 1775 Gordon married Joanna (usually known as "Jackie") Trotter, daughter of Thomas Trotter of the adjacent estate of Mortonhall. She predeceased Gordon by sixteen years. Soon after his marriage Gordon drew up plans for a new mansion-house in the Hermitage: this was designed in Adam style, perhaps by Robert Burn and was completed in 1785.

Charles Gordon, according to a *Times* obituary, "inherited all the penuriousness, if not all the ability of management, of his father". He is reported to have remained in bed as much as possible in order to avoid the necessity of spending money. His passion for saving, it was said, was a disease. He had three sons and three daughters. One of the latter, Joanna,

The family of Charles Gordon of Cluny and Braid, showing Hermitage of Braid House

Left to right: Cosmo, Alexander, Joanna ("Jackie"), Mary, Charlotte and John, heir to the title
Oil painting by Alexander Nasmyth, c.1790
By courtesy of Mr & Mrs R. A. C. Linzee-Gordon of Cluny
Photograph by kind permission of Dr J. C. B. Cooksey

familiarly called (as was her mother) "Jackie", acquired a somewhat bizarre and dramatic place in the tales of the Hermitage, and thereby in local Scottish history. A friend is on record as writing to another, referring to Jackie Gordon as being "ridiculously dressed". Nevertheless, as another commentator remarks, this did not prevent her "capturing" in May 1804 the future Earl of Stair, then Mr John Dalrymple. This had sad consequences, which ultimately, it is said, led to Jackie shutting herself up in Hermitage House in a state of acute mental derangement, her screams echoing in the steep-sided gorge of the Braid Burn. John Dalrymple, who was an officer in the Dragoon Guards, when he proposed marriage to Jackie, which she readily accepted,

insisted that they keep their promise to themselves until his father died and he succeeded to the title. So they exchanged letters of secret promise to each other, but Jackie's regular letters to her *fiancé* were eventually intercepted and returned. The Earl of Stair died on February 23rd 1807, and Jackie Gordon, believing the need for secrecy over, proceeded to publish her forthcoming marriage formally. But the new Earl had different plans. He had tired of Jackie Gordon, and in June 1808 married Miss Laura Manners, future Countess of Dysart. Jackie Gordon not unnaturally reacted swiftly and violently. Her case went to law and the secret pledges of the original betrothal were upheld as valid and she was declared to be the Countess of Stair, the gaining of this title being

221

undoubtedly her overriding desire.

The Earl of Stair tried other defences: Jackie Gordon's infidelity to him was one submission. But he was overruled. However, in June 1820, her marriage to the Earl was in fact annulled. Jackie nonetheless continued to call herself the Countess Dowager of Stair. Miss Manners, who had formally married the Earl of Stair, died in 1834, pre-deceasing her rival by thirteen years. The Earl himself became ill and was confined to his bed until his death in Paris in 1840. And the "Countess Dowager", proclaiming herself so until the end, died in February 1847, but in her last days was a tormented, mentally deranged lady. The words on her tombstone in the elaborate Gordon burial place in St Cuthbert's church-yard described her as "Joanna Gordon, Countess of Stair".

Charles Gordon of Cluny and Braid died on May 15th 1814. In 1878 the lands of Braid passed from a descendant, John Gordon, to his widow, who married Sir Reginald Cathcart. Their heirs were Mr and Mrs Linzee-Gordon of Cluny Castle, Aberdeenshire, who owned, in addition to Braid, the lands of Midmar. Eventually much of the original Braid estate had been sold off for the building of what R. L. Stevenson called "villadom". The present descendants of Charles Gordon of Cluny and Braid are Mr and Mrs Robin Linzee-Gordon, of Cluny Castle, who kindly suggested much of the source material for this research.

SIR JOHN SKELTON

WHEN Sir John Skelton took up residence in the Hermitage of Braid in 1868, this beautifully situated mansion-house was at last to enter a new era of peace and cultural tranquillity more in keeping than hitherto with the atmosphere of seclusion and retreat suggested by its name. For long the steep wooded slopes rising above the valley traversed by the Braid Burn had witnessed and echoed to events of tragedy, violence and despair. Sir William Dick of Braid, 17th-century owner, and of legendary wealth, had gone from Braid to die a pauper's death in a London debtor's prison. Later, in Robert Fairlie's time, an armed attack took place on the owner, and during the ownership of the miserly Charles Gordon the house had become a bleak self-imposed prison for his hapless daughter "Jackie" whose demented screams repelled chance visitors. During Sir John Skelton's residence for nearly thirty years the mansion-house echoed to the peaceful sounds of the scintillating dinner-table conversations of the many famous writers and poets who came to reside happily at the Hermitage as Skelton's guests.

Sir John Skelton
Drawing by Sir Noel Paton

Sir John Skelton was born in Edinburgh in 1831, son of James Skelton of Sandford, Newton, Writer to the Signer, and Sheriff-substitute of Peterhead where John was brought up. He was educated at Edinburgh University, and in 1854 became an Advocate. While his career lay in law and public administration, it was his literary talents which eventually attracted wide attention and praise. Skelton's distinguished service in public life included the secretaryship, and later chairmanship, of the Scottish Board of Supervision, which later became the Scottish Local Government Board. This appointment was prompted by Disraeli of whom he wrote an essay in tribute. He carried out much notable work in the administration of the new Public Health legislation of 1867 and in the application of Poor Law, and wrote much authoritative work in these fields.

Apart from notable authorship on social questions, Skelton began to make an impression in the wider literary world by his contributions to *Blackwood's Magazine* with which he maintained a long association. In 1876 there appeared his major and important work on a controversial historical subject: *The Impeachment of Mary, Queen of Scots*, a scholarly defence of the hapless queen, and in 1887 *Maitland of Lethington and the Scotland of Mary, Queen of Scots*. Among his other prolific works, best known were his *Essays of Shirley* and *Table Talk of Shirley*. This latter highly entertaining collection consists mainly of Skelton's reminiscences of the visits of his guests at the Hermitage. These included Anthony Froude, Dante Gabriel Rossetti, Robert Browning, Thomas Carlyle, and Thomas Huxley. Correspondence reveals that while the dinner-table conversations were no doubt erudite and highly charged with literary brilliance they were also occasions for high spirits. Thomas Huxley on one occasion remarked that he would wear the kilt in order to be as little dressed as possible! Many of the guests recalled their pleasure in the unique surroundings of the Hermitage and the great and kind hospitality of Sir John and Lady Skelton.

Among Skelton's innumerable reminiscences is that of an evening walk with the famous Edinburgh University Principal Tulloch across what was then open country to Swanston Cottage. Young R.L.S. was not at home but Mrs Stevenson gave the visitors some of her son's work to take away for comment. Tulloch read it next morning at the breakfast table and wrote later of his excitement at discovering "a fresh voice with a note delicate and unborrowed as the lark".

Sir John Skelton was much involved in the local community. He was a member of Christ's Scottish Episcopal Church at Holy Corner, and wrote a short history of this church. He was also amongst those, including his nearby neighbour Sir John Forrest of Comiston, who campaigned for the abolition of road tolls in Scotland; their abolition duly took place in 1883. Five years later Skelton arranged for the then obsolete toll-house at the foot of Morningside Road, beside the Briggs o' Braid over the Jordan Burn, to be carefully taken down and rebuilt at the entrance to the Hermitage in Braid Road. There it still stands. While there is no historical evidence of there ever having been a hermitage, as such, in the Braid estate, at one period during Sir John Skelton's residence a man did make his home in a little cave on a sloping bank, sleeping on a bed of leaves. Skelton allowed the man to remain and treated him with great kindness and courtesy.

Sir John Skelton died at the Hermitage of Braid on July 19th 1897. His widow Anne, daughter of James Adair Laurie, Professor of Surgery in Glasgow University, remained with their several children at the Hermitage until 1922.

PROFESSOR CHARLES G. BARKLA

Professor Charles G. Barkla

RESIDENTS at the Hermitage of Braid have left their mark upon their life and times, ever since the almost legendary days of the Knights of Brad or Breda — the possible origin of the district's name — the 12th-century loyal servants of William the Lion. The incredibly dramatic and tragic life of the merchant and Lord Provost William Dick, from the heyday of his prosperity as an ultra-wealthy businessman until his death in a London debtors' prison; the clash of swords and the sound of muskets in Fairlie's day; the great development of the estate and fine new mansion-house under Charles Gordon of Cluny; right up to the peaceful pastoral idyllic atmosphere of Sir John Skelton's era, when the ancient figures of the Knights were replaced by their latter-day counter-parts — the leading figures of the literary and artistic world; and the echoes of the demented screams of the hapless "Jackie" Gordon faded in the memory, charmed away by the calm and cultured tones of Skelton's dinner guests. But in the early 1920s yet another very different, and at that time very modern, era was repre-sented by the residence in the Hermitage, together with his family, of one of the world's truly great scientists of the age, whose researches earned for him the Nobel Prize in Physics.

Charles Glover Barkla was born on June 7th 1877, at Widnes in Lancashire, of a family of Cornish extraction, from which his surname derives. His father was Secretary of the Atlas Chemical Company of Widnes. Educated first at the Liverpool Institute and then at University College, Liverpool and after specialising in experimental physics under the famous Sir Oliver Lodge, as was common for those who had excelled in the subject; Charles Barkla set out for Cambridge and entered Trinity College, in 1899, as a research

224

student in physics. However, science was not Barkla's only interest or source of distinction. He also had an amazing bass voice of seemingly unique power and quality. After one year at Trinity College, therefore, he transferred to King's College, simply to become a member of its famous choir under the esteemed Dr Mann. He gained much honour for his solo parts, which could be relied upon to ensure a full attendance at chapel. Indeed, so remarkable, apparently, was his voice that more than one music critic forecast a distinguished future for him as a singer and questioned whether to continue in physics would not mean sacrificing his real vocation in the musical world. Charles Barkla decided, however, to pursue both callings.

At Cambridge he worked in the famous Cavendish Laboratory under J. J. Thomson, and with notable colleagues, who included Lord Rutherford. Through the prompting of Thomson he embarked on the research which was to bring him renown. The eminent physicist, Professor Max Born, later a professorial colleague with Barkla at Edinburgh University, praised his work and pointed out that so thorough had been Röntgen's own work following his discovery of X-rays that Barkla's further research in that field constituted the most important addition to the knowledge of them since their discovery. Professor Sir Edmund Whittaker described Barkla as "the most distinguished representative of experimental work in the Scottish professoriate". Barkla's discoveries marked a new epoch in physics. The nature of his work is highly specialised and technical, of course,

and has been fully described elsewhere.

In recognition of his truly outstanding contributions to physics Barkla received many honours. In 1909 he was appointed Professor of Physics at King's College, London, and in 1913 was appointed to the Chair of Natural Philosophy at Edinburgh University. In 1917 Barkla was awarded the Nobel Prize in Physics, and in the same year the Hughes Medal of the Royal Society, of which he had been made a Fellow in 1912. In 1977 the Swedish Government, to commemorate the sixty years since Professor Barkla's Nobel award, in a unique gesture of appreciation issued a special postage stamp bearing the distinguished prizewinner's profile against the background of Edinburgh's Old College.

In Edinburgh University Professor Barkla's classes in physics, which were unusually large, required the professor to be an outstanding lecturer: Barkla's magnificent voice still rich in the resonance of King's College choir days, and his commanding presence, ensured crowded and appreciative lecture theatres.

Professor Charles G. Barkla
By courtesy of his daughter, Mrs Cecile M. C. Paterson

Although his research interests in X-rays were primarily of a "pure science" nature Barkla was well aware of their practical implications for medical diagnosis and treatment. On several occasions abroad he had met Madame Curie. He was a deeply religious man, of the Methodist faith, and his fine voice made a rich contribution to hymns of praise in Nicholson Square Church. He saw in the pursuit of science "an investigation as part of the quest for God the Creator", and his discoveries as an extension of his religious awareness. He married Mary Esther Cowell, daughter of John T. Cowell, Receiver General of the Isle of Man. They had three sons and one daughter. Barkla's most satisfying relaxation was to be with his family, either travelling or simply enjoying the beautiful surroundings of the Hermitage of Braid, which they reluctantly had to leave in 1938. The sudden death, while on active service in Carthage in August 1943, of his youngest son, Flight-Lieutenant Michael Barkla, M.B., Ch.B., Ettles Scholar in his final year in Medicine, and who had shown early signs of a distinguished career in surgery, reminiscent of his father's academic achievements, was a source of deep grief to Professor Barkla in what proved to be the last year of his life, and despite an apparently satisfactory recovery from an operation he died at his home "Braidwood" in Corrennie Gardens, near the Hermitage, on 23rd October 1944. During Professor Barkla's residence at the Hermitage, the dining-room echoed to the discussions of some of the world's leading scientists, who were his frequent guests, as had been the many notable *littérateurs* of Sir John Skelton's day.

JOHN McDOUGAL

EDINBURGH'S citizens have cause to be grateful to very many benefactors for generous gifts which enhance their leisure time and other interests, and lovers of nature and wild life must surely be especially grateful to one South Edinburgh resident. His donation half a century ago of a "public park" (its official designation originally, though never seeming quite appropriate) continues to bring pleasure to countless people of all ages and at all seasons of the year. The benefactor was Mr John Mc-Dougal and his gift to the city nothing less than the unique natural wonderland of the Hermitage of Braid itself.

The Hermitage provides yet another example of a place concerning which a great deal is known, as regards its history, its natural features of wild flowers, birds and animals and flora — yet concerning its generous donor information is sadly all too sparse. A native of Edinburgh, Mr John McDougal was educated at Melville College, formerly known as Edinburgh Institution and now merged with Daniel Stewart's College. In 1898 he became a partner with Mr John Herdman in the firm of Herdman and McDougal, Grain Importers, Leith. After his retiral from business Mr McDougal, who remained unmarried, bought the estate of Crochmore, Irongray, near Dumfries, where he lived with his brother.

After his brother's death in 1930 Mr McDougal returned to Edinburgh, residing at No 27 Cluny Drive, in Morningside. He indicated to his friend, Lord Provost Louis S. Gumley, that he intended bequeath-

Mr John McDougal

is seen 6th from right (wearing "plus fours") during handing over ceremony to City of Edinburgh of rustic shelter at Blackford Pond in June 1938

Photograph by courtesy of "Scotsman" Publications Ltd.

ing a sum of money to the city sufficient to purchase the Hermitage of Braid from the Cluny Trustees. The sum of £10,000 was mentioned, but the Lord Provost persuaded Mr McDougal to acquire the Hermitage during his own life-time and present it to the civic authorities. This Mr McDougal did. The official ceremony during which he conveyed his generous gift to the Lord Provost — "for the use and enjoyment of the citizens" — took place at a gathering in front of the Hermitage of Braid House, which was, of course, included in the purchase, on June 10th 1938. Mr McDougal also presented a sundial in the form of an astrolabe and ancillary sphere, beautifully wrought in bronze by Messrs Henshaw and set on a stone pedestal a little distant from and in front of the house. Professor Charles Barkla and his family, the last private tenants of Hermitage House, remained in residence until the transfer of ownership to the city was finalised. Mr McDougal spent many pleasant days in the Hermitage towards the end of his life, deriving much pleasure from sitting near the house, as an anonymous observer, watching people enjoying the delightful amenities. He died at his home in Cluny Drive on August 1st 1949, aged 87. In accordance with his own wish his ashes were scattered in the Hermitage on August 5th at a private ceremony attended by relatives and Lord Provost Andrew Murray. In more recent years the Hermitage of Braid has become a Countryside Information Centre, with specially trained staff, and is under further re-development.

ELIZABETH BURNET

JUST off Braid Hills Drive, which affords one of the most magnificent panoramic views of Edinburgh, and standing on the south bank high above the deeply set valley of the Hermitage of Braid, is the sturdy old farm-house of Upper Braid, long since comfortably modernised inside and known also as Nether Braid or Over Braid. Above the main doorway on the north side of the house is carved the date 1794. Four years earlier than this there occurred in this finely situated house an event which brought great sadness in "high society" circles in Edinburgh, but particularly deeply to the heart of Robert Burns, and inspired him to write a special elegy. Here, at that time far out from the city, on June 15th 1790, Elizabeth Burnet — Burns's "Fair Burnet" — daughter of the learned and eccentric Scottish judge Lord Monboddo, died of tuberculosis at the early age of 24.

Soon after Burns's arrival in Edinburgh in 1786 and when he was beginning to receive many invitations into the city's exclusive and sophisti-

"Fair Burnet"

Elizabeth Burnet is seen 3rd from left at social occasion in her father's house in St John's Street. Robert Burns is on her left

Drawing by James Edgar

By courtesy of the National Galleries of Scotland, Edinburgh

cated literary circles, he was introduced by Sir Henry Erskine to Lord Monboddo through their close links in Freemasonry. The judge was a philosopher and author of considerable repute (having once merited a visit from the famous lexicographer Dr Samuel Johnson) and to be invited to his highly select house-parties in his home at 13 St John Street, off the Canongate, was indeed a privilege and an honour.

Sir Walter Scott recorded in after years that "the best society, whether in respect of rank or literary distinction, was always to be found there". The guests sat down at a candle-lit and flower-strewn table and had the choicest wines poured into their glasses from rose-garlanded decanters of Grecian pattern.

Burns soon became a regular guest and quickly fell under the spell of the judge's beautiful and highly intelligent daughter, who had spurned offers of marriage from many of Edinburgh's leading and most hand-some men, including the distinguished Professor James Gregory, later of Canaan Lodge; she chose to remain her father's devoted housekeeper.

In his *Address to Edinburgh* Burns wrote:

Thy daughters bright thy walks adorn,
Gay as the gilded summer sky,
Sweet as the dewy milk-white thorn,
Dear as the raptur'd thrill of joy!
Fair Burnet strikes th'adoring eye,
Heav'ns beauties on my fancy shine:
I see the sire of love on high,
And own His work indeed divine.

The poet also wrote: "There has not been anything nearly like her in all the combinations of beauty, grace and goodness, the great Creator has formed, since Milton's Eve on the first day of her existence".

When Elizabeth Burnet contracted tuberculosis she was sent to live in Braid farmhouse on account of its healthy situation, fresh air, good farm produce and other factors considered therapeutic for the

228

disease in those days. Burns, who is known to have walked over the Braid Hills on several occasions with his friend Dugald Stewart and with Alexander Nasmyth, the artist, may have visited Elizabeth Burnet at Braid during her illness. But the hoped-for salutary atmosphere of the farm-house was of no avail, and she died.

After her death, in a letter to Alexander Cunningham, Burns wrote: "I have these several months been hammering at an elegy on the amiable and accomplished Miss Burnet. I have got, and can get, no further than the following fragment". Again he wrote: "I had the honour of being pretty well acquainted with her and have seldom felt so much at the loss of an acquaintance as when I heard that so amiable and accomplished a piece of God's work was no more". This was the elegy he had "been hammering at" for months:

Life ne'er exulted in so rich a prize
As Burnet, lovely from her native skies;
Nor envious death so triumphed in a blow.
As that which laid th' accomplish'd Burnet low.

Thy form and mind, sweet maid, can I forget?
In richest are the brightest jewels set!
In thee high Heaven above was truest shown.
As by his noblest work the Godhead best is known.

Then in reference to the Hermitage of Braid with its wooded deep gorge carrying the Braid Burn, the farm of Upper Braid standing high up on the south bank, Burns continued:

In vain ye flaunt in summer's pride, ye groves;
Thou crystal streamlet with thy flowing shore,
Ye woodland choir that chant your idle loves,
Ye cease to charm — Eliza is no more!
The parent's heart that nestled fond in thee.
That heart how sunk, a prey to grief and care;
So deck'd the woodbine sweet, yon aged tree;
So from it ravaged, leaves it bleak and bare.

Such was the effect upon Burns of the death of "Fair Burnet" in the sturdy farm-house which may still be seen today. And such the disastrous effect upon her father, Lord Monboddo, that he kept her portrait draped in black until his own death in 1799.

THE CLERKS OF PENICUIK AND THE BUCKSTANE

OF the many relics from the past scattered about Morningside and its vicinity one of the most ancient is the Buckstane, which stands on the east side of Braid Road a short distance beyond Mortonhall Golf Club's club-house. It is placed there in a prominent position at the gates to the old Buckstane farmhouse, and with an appropriately inscribed plaque above. In essence the story is that in far-off times the Scottish kings, riding out by this old direct Roman road from the south to the hunt on the lower slopes of the Pentland Hills, unleashed their buckhounds here at the stone. Unlike the so-called "bore stone" on the wall outside

Morningside Parish Church at Churchhill, which had no bore or deep hole imprinted in it, the Buckstane did have such a hole, in which it is believed was hoisted the royal standard to indicate that the King was hunting in the area.

Sir John Clerk, 2nd Baronet of Penicuik
by William Aikman
Reproduced from his Memoirs: 1676-1755

In the days of Robert the Bruce, the story continues, during the hunt, some distance southwards on the Pentlands near Glencorse, the King was frequently menaced by a swift white deer. He challenged his nobles to see if their dogs could corner the animal where his own had failed. Sir William St Clair of Roslin and Penicuik accepted the challenge, pledging his life that his two dogs "Help" and "Hold" would succeed. Praying earnestly to St Katherine for her aid, Sir William slipped his dogs and after almost giving up hope, for the deer seemed once again to be escaping, suddenly and swiftly his dogs attacked and brought it to ground. Bruce, in delight, embracing Sir William St Clair, granted him as a reward, in freehold, substantial lands nearby. The condition upon which he was to hold the lands was that whenever in time to come a Scottish monarch should pass by the Buckstane *en route* to hunt in the vicinity, he or his descendants must appear at the stone and as the King — or Queen — passed, give three blasts on a hunting-horn. The ancient condition is still binding upon Sir John Clerk of Penicuik to the present day.

After the original hunting incident the much relieved Sir William St Clair in thanksgiving to "St Katherine of the Hopes", built in her honour a chapel at the east end of what is now Glencorse Reservoir, the ruins of which may occasionally be seen in time of drought. Lest all this should seem pure legend, strange to relate the Royal Commission on the Ancient and Historical Monuments of Scotland in their Inventory of 1929 for the County of Midlothian refers to the ruined chapel as having been visited in 1915 and suggests the 13th century — the time of Robert the Bruce — as the probable period of its construction.

Now it is not possible to obtain any greater detail concerning the Sir William St Clair to whom were originally gifted the lands "beside Pentland Moor", nor to trace his portrait. Nearly four centuries were to elapse before his successor Sir John Clerk, 2nd Baronet of Penicuik, in an early chapter of his journals of 1676-1755 deals in some detail with his ancestors and in particular refers to a deed of 1591 conferring "the succession of Andrew Penycuikis" to his father, Sir John, 1st Baronet, with a condition of "Six blasts of a flowing horn, on the common mure of Edinburgh . . . at the King's hunt on the said mure . . ". A footnote points out that the reference to six blasts is probably a misprint, three being the traditional number. Sir Walter Scott mentions the tenure of the Baronet of Penicuik's land "by blast of bugle free".

Of the many successors to the Sir William St Clair of the Bruce story, the Sir John Clerk referred to above as 2nd Baronet of Penicuik has perhaps earned a place of special interest in many spheres. He was a very notable scholar, and his diaries are a rich source of information, concerning his education in the parish school of Penicuik, at Glasgow University and afterwards at Leyden; of the current affairs of his day; and of his extensive travels in Europe, including Vienna, Florence, Rome and Paris between 1694 and 1699, where he met leading scholars, poets, artists and musicians of the time. In 1699 he returned to Scotland, and a year later was admitted to the Scottish Bar. He was elected a member of the Scottish Parliament for the Burgh of Whithorn from 1702 until the Union, and a Member of the first British Parliament. He observed how opposed the Scottish people were to the Union of the Parliaments. For a time the future Lord Provost George Drummond of Edinburgh was Lord Clerk's amanuensis. His recreation included curling at the original Penicuik House, where he generally resided, and where he wrote extensively on history, philosophy, poetry, the classics, and antiquarian subjects. He carried out much important excavation of Roman remains in the area. The Society of Antiquaries and the Royal Society of Edinburgh elected him to membership. He died on October 4th 1755.

JAMES S. BENNET

Mr James Bennet, F.S.A.

Seen holding the Scottish Lion Rampant flag after the unveiling of the resited Buckstane in 1964. On extreme right: Sir John Clerk of Penicuik holding ancient hunting horn
Photograph by courtesy of Mr Bennets' daughter, Mrs Margaret E. Fraser, Kiltarlity

IF the family of the Clerks of Penicuik are inseparably associated with the history of the Buckstane, and still remain bound by the obligation to sound three blasts upon the horn, seated on or near the stone, their task would be made more feasible by the deep interest and enterprising action of a Morningside resident of some years ago. He was responsible for having the Buckstane moved from its original, somewhat inconspicuous, site on the west side of Braid Road and set prominently some yards further southwards on the other side of the road, outside the gateway to the old Buckstane farmhouse. This man was Mr James Bennet, FSA, author of an invaluable little booklet on the history of the Buckstane, published by Edinburgh City Libraries in 1964 and still on sale.

James Spalding Bennet was born in 1892, second son of the manager of the Co-operative Store at Ratho in Midlothian. Educated at George Heriot's School, where he was *dux* in handicrafts, James Bennet trained as an architect after the award of a scholarship to the Edinburgh College of Art. At the outbreak of the First World War he abandoned this career to enlist in the Royal Scots. His training in surveying was put to good use for he transformed the information obtained from aerial survey photographs to replace the outmoded French maps previously used by the troops. For this service he was awarded the *Croix de Guerre* at the end of the war. After demobilisation he returned to being a draughtsman and in 1931 set up his own practice, working mainly on church buildings. In the Second World War he was appointed in charge of historic buildings requisitioned for military purposes. After the war Mr Bennet was involved in the restoration of parts of the Royal Mile, especially the renovation of the Canongate Tolbooth.

At the end of the Great War Mr Bennet had married Miss Helen Ross Tanner, third daughter of Samuel Tanner, market gardener at Plewlands nursery, Morningside, and later at Hillwood Mains, Ratho. Early in their married life Mr Bennet and his wife acquired the deserted farm-house of Buckstane, converting it into a delightful family house and the old farmyard nearby into an imaginative garden. The remarkable patches of brilliant red poppies which flourished in the garden owed their origin to the transfer of old flagstones of 1785. For Mr and Mrs Bennet and their family of one daughter and

two sons Buckstane farmhouse was for long a most pleasant "country residence", relatively far out from the city.

In due course Mr Bennet set himself what he regarded as a primary task. Two hundred and fifty yards to the north, up Braid Road on the opposite west side, was the ancient Buckstane, standing outside the wall of a private dwelling-house and apparently doomed to remain obscure and unnoticed. Mr Bennet thought its history deserved to be better known. He therefore obtained permission to transfer the stone to its present site near the gateway to the old farm-house. A fine bronze plaque recounting the history was placed on the wall and the official ceremony of re-siting it took place in 1964, in the presence of civic officials and of Sir John Clerk, 10th Baronet of Penicuik, and Lady Clerk, Sir John being the descendant of St Clair of Roslin and Penicuik of the original hunting incident centuries ago, he who still has the obligation to sound the three blasts.

Robert Louis Stevenson had associations with Buckstane farmhouse: he refers to it in a few lines in one of his nostalgic poems: "I gang nae mair where aince I gaed, by Buckstane, Fairmilehead and Braid ..."; and Mr Bennet, aware of this, could not rest content until he had visited Monterey and Pebble Beach in California where once Stevenson had been well known.

An ordained elder of the then St Matthew's Church in Braid Road, Mr Bennet gave much professional architectural advice to the Kirk Session as regards the conservation of this very fine building. Ten years after his wife's death Mr Bennet left

Edinburgh for Foyers in Inverness-shire to reside with his younger son, Dr Arthur Bennet. There he died, aged 92. Those interested in the history of the Buckstane, its preservation, and in the surrounding district, owe much to the enthusiastic dedication of James Bennet.

6 · MORTONHALL/ FAIRMILEHEAD

THOMAS TROTTER, 7TH BARONET OF MORTONHALL

Thomas Trotter 7th Baronet of Mortonhall

by courtesy of Major A. J. Trotter of Mortonhall

NEARLY seven centuries ago the ancient lands of Mortonhall, centred on the north side of Frogston Road East, were among the substantial possessions of that venerable family the St Clairs of Roslin. Many centuries earlier the district was the scene of a Roman camp. In 1635 the extensive area of Mortonhall became the property of John Trotter, and he became the first Baron of Mortonhall. Thereafter the lands became inextricably associated with this family. They were already the proprietors, as they remain today, of

Catchelraw and Charterhall in the Borders. Each of the successive Barons of Mortonhall contributed his own chapter to the long history of the family. John, the first, was noted for his Royalist sympathies, and was also a man of great charity and generosity, one of his many gifts being "the establishment in the College of Edinburgh of two bursars in philosophy". He died in 1641 aged 88 and was buried in the family vault in Greyfriars churchyard at the north wall. He left a great deal of money to the city, along with bequests to St Paul's Hospital for the poor in Leith Wynd, and Trinity Hospital nearby. John Trotter's son, of the same name, the second Baron, was also an ardent Royalist, and was fined £500 for allowing the Marquis of Montrose and his troops to camp on his land.

When in 1763 Henry Trotter succeeded as 7th Baron he had already arranged with his younger brother John that another younger brother, Thomas, would in fact bear the title. At this time the original house at Mortonhall was probably a fort-like structure, surrounded by a moat with a drawbridge, and it was Thomas Trotter who, in 1765, had this early dwelling demolished and commissioned the noted architect John Baxter, junior, to build the fine tall Georgian house in 1769 which remains today, having served many purposes since last it was a family residence.

Prior to his succession to Mortonhall Thomas Trotter was a merchant

234

and brewer in Edinburgh, and for the latter trade rented for a period the Tailors' Hall in the Cowgate. The output of this brewery seems to have averaged about 120 barrels per month. Among the list of his customers on record was "The Castle of Edinburgh", which placed quite substantial orders. In addition to possessing Mortonhall and the family estates in the Borders, Thomas Trotter also acquired the lands and barony of Eyemouth, which included the harbour and village along with farmlands and Wedderburn mill and farm.

Trotter was a man of many interests and activities. He had been elected an Edinburgh City Councillor in 1742 and was later appointed a bailie. At that time he lived in the Canongate and worshipped in the Tron Kirk. He seems to have been a shrewd businessman, and records remain which detail his Canongate household financial budget along with particulars of servants' wages and those of his brewery workers. At one period, when his brother lived with him, he charged him £10 for board and lodgings over a five-month stay. However, his paying guest must have appreciated the hospitality provided since he paid his brother £21 extra as a gift. Despite so many commitments, he found relaxation in playing golf several times a week at Leith Links. He was a member of the Honourable Company of Edinburgh golfers.

In June 1743 Thomas Trotter had married Miss Joanna Porterfield of Hapland in Ayrshire, then aged 16. His account-book records purchase of a diamond engagement ring costing £7.15.0. They had seven sons and eight daughters. The family's medical attendants were two notable Edinburgh doctors of that time, Dr Nathaniel Spens and Dr Porterfield. Although his wife's name was Joanna, Thomas Trotter always called her "Jackie". It was one of his daughters named Joanna, but again known as "Jackie", whom Charles Gordon of Cluny married in 1775; and another of Gordon's daughters, who was involved in the unhappy and tempestuous romance with the Earl of Stair, which caused her eventual insanity, was also called "Jackie". When Thomas Trotter died in 1792 and his widow was given the choice of residing in one of the dower-houses, either at Swanston or Blackford, she chose the latter and lived there for 22 years. She died in 1814, aged 86. Later Miss Menie Trotter, one of her daughters, came to reside at Blackford, and this interesting lady, "who bathed daily in the Jordan which flowed past her house", has been described in an earlier chapter. Thomas Trotter and his wife were interred in the Greyfriars family vault.

OLIVER CROMWELL

IN 1507, and perhaps again in 1513, Canaan was honoured by visits from James IV. Two centuries earlier the Braid Hills were chosen as a brief resting-place by England's Edward I before and after his defeat by Sir William Wallace at the Battle of Falkirk in 1298. Edward III likewise is said to have chosen to camp on the Braids while continuing his predecessors' attempts to subdue the Scots. These hills seem to have been favoured on account of their

Oliver Cromwell

commanding and perhaps almost impregnable position high above the city. In 1650 yet another important historical personage, though most certainly not a "Royal", also chose to visit South Edinburgh and to encamp on what a writer much later called "the furzy hills of Braid". This was the mighty Protector himself, Oliver Cromwell, whose troops, 16,000 of them it is said, following their victory at the Battle of Dunbar, occupied the gently-rising Gallachlaw above the site of today's Princess Margaret Rose Hospital and described in certain records "as betwixt Braid Crags and the Pentland Hills". According to Thomas Whyte, the historian of nearby Liberton, which in early times included the Mortonhall estate and the Galachllaw, the latter of Roman origin, from the days of a large Roman settlement in this vicinity, and the name meant "fortitude or valour"; and it was upon the Gallachlaw they held their courts of justice. Other historians have derived the name from the "Gallows Law" or "Gallows Hill", the place where Cromwell hanged local rebels and some of his own soldiers found guilty of looting. It is recorded that when one of Cromwell's sergeants was condemned for some offence "there was no tree to hang him on". Trees in profusion now pleasantly cover the Gallachlaw.

In Thomas Whyte's day local people apparently pointed out a rectangular rampart on top of the Gallachlaw as "Oliver's Camp", the troops having encamped on the lower slopes. Claims have been made of relics of Cromwell's occupation having been discovered. As regards Morningside's Biblical names, certain historians have suggested that these probably originated as a result of the Protector's troops going down to forage in that area where certainly one location was known as "Egypt". Perhaps meeting with resistance from the local inhabitants, Cromwell's men, who were habitually citing Biblical phrases, may have reported that their skirmishes in "Egypt" might be likened to "Joshua against the Canaanites"; in the course of time other such names followed.

DR T. RATCLIFFE BARNETT AND WILLIAM A. COCHRANE, FRCS(Ed.)

PERHAPS most modern hospitals and similar institutions are now founded by the collective decision of a government department, local

236

Rev. Dr T. Ratcliffe Barnett

by courtesy of his daughter, Miss Janet Ratcliffe Barnett

"The Edinburgh Hospital for Crippled Children" would be re-named as above, this was in honour of the Princess but, of course, she was not the foundress.

If, as might have been the case in an earlier era, the hospital had been named after the two men who had originally conceived the need for it and worked to make their ideal a reality, it might properly have been named the Barnett-Cochrane Orthopaedic Hospital, since the foundation of what was to become such a highly important hospital with a world-wide reputation was initially the dream of two friends, each distinguished in his own right: Dr T. Ratcliffe Barnett, DD, from 1914 to 1938 Minister of Greenbank Church, and Mr William Alexander Cochrane, FRCS (Ed.), a surgeon of great dedication and skill.

authority or community organisa-tion, with the influence or role of an individual occupying a minor place and the funding required coming from official sources. It was not always so, as innumerable such places of great fame remind us, bearing the name of the founder or of the person who met the initial (and sometimes the continuing) cost. Many of Edinburgh's best known fee-paying schools still bear the names of their founders, albeit their original conditions for entry, or the nature of the institutions themselves have greatly changed. Perhaps the important, and well-known, Princess Margaret Rose Orthopaedic Hospital in point of time falls somewhere in between. Though in 1933 it was agreed that what had previously been known as

Mr William Cochrane, F.R.C.S.(E).

By courtesy of the Princess Margaret Rose Hospital, Edinburgh

Photograph by T. Tyrell

The origins of the Princess Margaret Rose Hospital, as an idea at any rate, lie in another hospital, Bangour, where Dr Ratcliffe Barnett and Mr William Cochrane first met by chance. Mr Cochrane, after a distinguished undergraduate career in Medicine at Edinburgh University culminating with first class honours in 1915, served as a Captain in the Royal Army Medical Corps from 1916 to 1920. He was wounded in France in 1917 and transferred to the Edinburgh War Hospital at Bangour, where, although still on crutches, his hands and to that extent his surgical skills being unaffected, he assisted Sir Robert James and Sir Harold Stiles.

During his last fifteen months at Bangour he had charge of 100 surgical beds with all the operations and post-operative care which that involved. It was in the course of his Bangour duties that he first met the hospital chaplain, the Reverend T. Ratcliffe Barnett, and soon a deep and abiding friendship developed. Both shared a consuming concern for crippled people, especially the children who were thus sadly afflicted. Perhaps in the hospital cafeteria they first discussed their ideal: the foundation of a hospital in Edinburgh devoted entirely to the care and treatment of crippled children.

For the Reverend Dr Ratcliffe Barnett the care of crippled young people was no new or merely sentimental idea. In Greenbank Church in 1919, after the end of the First World War, at Dr Barnett's suggestion, a group of fit young men set out to revive a club previously run by the Crippled Aid Society in their premises in George Street, behind St Andrew's Church. The Greenbank men responded, and the George Street Club soon attracted boys over the age of fifteen and men up to the age of forty, most of whom on account of their disability were also unemployed. The Reverend Ratcliffe Barnett himself, although a very busy man and prolific author, attended this club weekly for many years. Hence the foundation of a new orthopaedic hospital would be for him the culmination of a long-standing practical concern and ideal.

However pressing the need for such a hospital, the idea had "to be sold" and substantial funds needed to be raised. As a prominent member of the Edinburgh Rotary Club Dr Barnett addressed his fellow-members in November 1925 on "The Problem of the Crippled Child", and he appealed for support for a new hospital. The response of the Rotary Club was immediate. A sum of £1,500 was quickly raised to finance a future planning inquiry. An executive group of prominent Edinburgh citizens was formed to find the initial £70,000 required to build a hospital of 75 beds. Other steps soon followed. A public conference in the City Chambers was held in March 1926 and a campaign launched. Surveys were carried out into the needs of crippled children for care and treatment, and these revealed that in Edinburgh, Fife, and South-East Scotland there were a vast number of deserving cases. Gradually the money came in. There was steady support from people at all levels. The detailed story has been told in a booklet published not long ago. The foundation stone was laid by the then Duchess of York on August 1st 1929, and the hospital's

238

first phase was opened on June 10th 1933. In the last half-century what was originally "The Edinburgh Hospital for Crippled Children" has become a general orthopaedic hospital of great and wide reputation.

The names of staff associated with the "P.M.R.'s" development are too numerous to single out, save for one man, Mr William Alexander Cochrane, the first surgeon appointed, whose skill and Herculean labours ensured steady progress, recruitment and sound training of staff — medical, nursing and auxiliary — together over the years creating the "P.M.R." atmosphere and spirit which transcends description. Willie Cochrane, as he was known to his colleagues, became a legend, and the extent of his contribution to the hospital which he had helped bring into being from an ideal to a reality is beyond measure. He was a pioneer of his subject in Scotland, being the country's first full-time orthopaedic surgeon. Alas, his valiant association with the P.M.R. was to be short-lived. He died on November 30th 1944, aged 51. A plaque in the hospital's vast main corridor commemorates his dedication and the affection in which he was held.

No one can have rejoiced so much to see his dream of the P.M.R. become a reality as the man who, despite so many interests, causes and activities, was primarily the devoted parish minister of Greenbank Church. Coming from St Andrew's Church Bo'ness to charges at Fala and Blackshiels, and in January 1914 to Greenbank, he found that his congregation worshipped in a makeshift hall while awaiting the building of a new church. After his war service the Reverend Ratcliffe Barnett returned to launch plans for the new church building, of very fine Gothic design by A. Lorne Campbell, and completed in 1927. A scholar and a prolific author of many books on the Scottish countryside, of which *The Road to Rannoch and the Summer Isles* and *Border By-ways and Lothian Lore* are perhaps best known, Dr Barnett knew well so many of the places as a walker. He was awarded a Doctorate of Philosophy by Edinburgh University in 1925. No man could have pleaded more reasons for keeping to his desk and his books, yet Dr Ratcliffe Barnett's Christianity implied total social commitment, and his unique part in the foundation of the Princess Margaret Rose Hospital is perhaps his best, if least known, memorial. He died on February 20th 1946, aged 77.

THE GAUGER'S FRIEND

SINCE the approximate date is known, and also where the farm-house stood until a few years ago, possibly some painstaking research might lead to the discovery of the name of the owner of Bowbridge whom Robert Louis Stevenson had in mind but referred to anonymously in the fascinating little anecdote which he related in the last few pages of his classic *Edinburgh: Picturesque Notes*. In the book's final chapter Stevenson described vividly how, viewed from Fairmilehead, on three sides Edinburgh slopes downwards — "to the sea, to the fat farms of Haddington, there to the mineral fields of Linlithgow. On the south alone it keeps rising. . . . For about

Bowbridge Farm, Near Fairmilehead
Pen and ink sketch by Henry Roy Westwood
By courtesy of Edinburgh City Libraries

two miles the road climbs upwards, a long hot walk in summer time. You reach the summit at a place where four roads meet beside the toll of Fairmilehead''. Stevenson's description of the fresh atmosphere of the district and of the view of Caerketton and Allermuir captures it all in words for ever.

Then begins his anecdote. Looking downhill southwards, "Below, over a stream, the road passes Bowbridge, now a dairy, but once a distillery of whisky". Some time here in the past century, Stevenson continues, the distiller was on good terms with the exciseman or gauger, whose duties required him at intervals to walk out from the city over the brow of Fairmilehead to assess and levy duty upon the Bowbridge stocks. The gauger was always sad that his good friend the distiller might — if caught unawares — have to pay quite heavily. With great compassion he found a tuneful way of warning his friends at Bowbridge of his imminent arrival. As he reached Fairmilehead, he produced from his pocket a flute which he always carried and, fitting its pieces together, ". . . set manfully to playing, as if for his own delectation and inspired by the beauty of the

scene. He had a favourite air, and this he always played, rather loudly, as he descended upon Bowbridge. It was 'Over the Hills and Far away'. The tune, and indeed the words, were not without their message and as his friend the distiller heard the melody growing louder he took action at the hint and, gathering most of his stock of Bowbridge whisky into barrels, he hurriedly loaded up his horse-drawn cart and set off speedily to Hillend where he buried (temporarily) in a prepared 'cupboard' in the hillside, his precious, if illegal, cargo."

Meantime, the distiller's wife had put a fat fowl on to roast and set a hospitable table in the back parlour. In due course the gauger arrived, rattled the door-knocker, and in a voice tinged with surprise at his arrival the good lady of the house greeted him amiably and invited him indoors. Inspection of his friend's modest stocks did not take long and the various papers were soon duly signed after the distiller, returned from Hillend, had slipped in by a back door. Everything being in order, a liberal but lawful dram was enjoyed all round and a fine meal followed. After all, the gauger had walked out all the way from the city to carry out his duties, and he surely deserved the best of hospitality. And, Stevenson goes on to relate, the meal over and the company in mellow mood, the gauger would entertain with a rendering of "Over the Hills and Far Away", while, with the exchange of knowing glances all round, everyone joined in heartily. Eventually, no doubt most properly fortified in spirit with "one for the road" (and a long road it was back to Edinburgh), the gauger would be seen receding into the distance towards Fairmilehead, and to his office, for the dutiful writing up of the requisite entries in his ledgers, as the notes from his flute grew ever fainter and fainter. Time for his hospitable friend to make his way back to Hillend to retrieve his cargo!

Such was the story that Stevenson wove around the old farmhouse of Bowbridge, which stood at the lowest point on the Biggar road on the banks of the Swanston Burn until alas it was swept away to permit the construction of a motorway. Bowbridge, gone physically perhaps but happily, like so much else in Edinburgh, immortalised by Stevenson's artistry in words.

7 · PLEWLANDS

MORNINGSIDE CEMETERY

THE fields of Plewlands or Plough-lands find a reference in the Protocol Book of James Young dated as early as March 23rd 1497. For long they were part of the estate of Braid. For nearly four centuries Plewlands remained open farmland with an extensive and important farm and substantial buildings appearing in early maps around 1800. It was not until 1882 that a plan was published for the proposed development of the area, which had been acquired by the Scottish Heritages Company Ltd. This plan provided small illustrations of various types of dwelling-houses which might be built and also showed the new street names proposed. Very much of this development duly took place. However, a very large area of the Plewlands estate was earmarked for the "Metropolitan Cemetery" and this "Garden of Rest", as William Mair describes it in his little book, had actually been opened in 1878. Mair draws attention to the then (at his time of writing, 1947), large numbers of very interesting people, Morningside residents and others, who had been interred in what became Morningside Cemetery.

In recent years, as a result of considerable house building by commercial companies which had taken place in the cemetery, for long privately owned, in certain instances threatening if not actually disturbing the privacy of graves, a survey was carried out by a Morningside lady and friends, in collaboration with the Scottish Genealogy Society, to

Inmates in the "uniform" of the Charity Workhouse

From "Old Edinburgh Characters and Costumes" by J. G. Howie c.1830-40 By courtesy of Edinburgh City Archives

ascertain more details of the numbers of people buried, their former places of residence, professions and other data. Consequently a great deal of extremely interesting and valuable information was brought to light. Survey revealed that amongst the very many people in Morningside's "Garden of Rest" are three Moderators of the General Assembly of the Church of Scotland; one Senator of the College of Justice; two Sheriffs; a former Principal and Vice-Chancellor of Edinburgh University as well as seven Professors; a former Vice-Chancellor of the Heriot Watt University; very many Fellows and Members of the Royal Society of Edinburgh; a former Chief Constable; authors, poets, artists, including Fellows and a former President of the Royal Scottish Academy; important public figures and personalities, many of whom gave their lives in the two World Wars, commemorated by Morningside's war memorial; and not least in a great mass burial area, without any

242

gravestones, thousands of people now unknown who died in the one-time City Poorhouse at Craiglockhart, the former Morningside Asylum, the old Royal Infirmary in Infirmary Street, and also from the former private surgical hospital in Chambers Street, originally established by Professor James Syme, which had become part of it. With so many people of greater or lesser interest, space prevents reference to more than but a few, and these are selected to illustrate something of the very wide range of people interred there and with all due respect and deference to those not mentioned.

ALISON CUNNINGHAM ("CUMMY")

Alison Cunningham ("Cummy")
By courtesy of the City of Edinburgh Museums

SUCH is the interest — world-wide — in Robert Louis Stevenson and not least in his famous childhood nurse, "Cummy", who is buried in Morningside Cemetery, that the question has arisen amongst certain Morningside groups as to whether a special plaque might be erected at the entrance-gate indicating the location of her grave. The absolute devotion of "Cummy" to her charge at Heriot Row, perhaps even in childhood showing signs to her, if then to no-one else, of his vivid creative imagination and genius, is well-known. And his indebtedness to her at that time and in so many ways is summed up above all in the lines which he wrote as the dedication to her of his famous *A Child's Garden of Verses*, published in 1884 and recalling his childhood across the years:

To Alison Cunningham from Her Boy

For the long nights you lay awake
And watched for my unworthy sake;
For your most comfortable hand
That led me through the uneven land:
For all the story books you read:
For all the pains you comforted:
For all you pitied, for all you bore,
In sad and happy days of yore:—
My second Mother, my first wife,
The angel of my infant life —
From the sick child now well and old,
Take, nurse, the little book you hold.

Lord Guthrie, one of Stevenson's almost innumerable biographers, in speculating on the sources of the writer's genius, enumerates the talents of his forebears — skilled engineers, a distinguished physician, a Biblical scholar — but he allows Stevenson to speak for himself: "They may talk about heredity", he wrote, "but if I inherited any literary talent, it was from 'Cummy'. It was she who gave me the first feeling for literature".

After having spent thirteen years with the Stevenson family at Swanston Cottage, and when Stevenson himself had married and gone to live in the South Seas, Cummy lived on in the little house at the gateway to Swanston Cottage together with her brother who was the tenant as a water department warden associated with the Swanston Springs tanks. An inscription on the doorway lintel indicates the dates. In 1893 Cummy left Swanston for a small flat at 23 Balcarres Street, where she lived happily with a succession of dogs, all of which died, it was said, from over-generous feeding. Then old age brought on increasing absent-mindedness and deafness and fear for her safety. At Balcarres Street many Stevenson devotees called on her, eager to hear her personal reminiscences of her protégé, and on one occasion, Lord Guthrie took her out to Swanston Cottage, where he then lived, to meet the Duchess of Sutherland and to be photographed with her. Finally, in need of constant care and companionship, she moved in with her cousin, Mrs Murdoch, at 1 Comiston Place, appreciatively but reluctant to admit the loss of her independence. There she slipped on the stairs and fractured a leg. Stevenson's widow, greatly concerned, cabled offers of every assistance for her care, but, having outlived her beloved Louis by twenty years, she died on July 21st 1913, aged 91. At the interment at Morningside Cemetery, in the presence of a few of her own and Stevenson's relatives and friends, a

Alison Cunningham's (Cummy's) Gravestone in Morningside Cemetery
Photograph by W. R. Smith

simple service was held. On her grave was placed a simple bunch of roses, honeysuckle and Canterbury bells from the garden of Swanston Cottage. The headstone reads: "In loving and grateful memory of Alison Cunningham, the beloved nurse of Robert Louis Stevenson".

ALEXANDER LOW BRUCE

IF "Cummy" was the intimate friend of one who wrote so vividly of imaginary adventure in near and far-off places, in another part of Morningside Cemetery is buried a man whose father-in-law experienced danger and adventure in distant Africa. This is Alexander Low Bruce, who married Agnes, daughter of the renowned explorer and medical missionary, Dr David Livingstone. But there is more to Bruce's

Alexander Low Bruce

the various events — probably the most impressive gathering ever held in the city's history — was the famous French chemist Louis Pasteur, whose researches into fermentation problems in the French wine industry had also led him on to his revolutionary discovery of the micro-organisms which caused disease and, with Dr Robert Koch of Germany, to become a pioneer in founding the science of bacteriology. Alexander Bruce was amongst those who persuaded Pasteur to come to Edinburgh when he was undecided about doing so, and when he did come arranged for him to visit Younger's premises at Holyrood and to give his expert advice on the brewing problems. This he did, with beneficial results.

Bruce, however, was also interested in Pasteur's researches in medical bacteriology and their implications for the study and control of infectious diseases, many of which were prevalent in Edinburgh. As a result of his meeting with Pasteur, who visited Bruce's family, expressing his respects to his wife on account of her famous father, Bruce altered his will, bequeathing £10,000 towards the foundation of the Usher Institute in Warrender Park Road, largely financed by Sir John Usher and devoted to the study of public health problems and their solution. Alexander Bruce died in 1893, after a sudden illness, aged only 54. He was buried in Morningside Cemetery, where his widow was later interred in April 1912. Bruce's death brought messages of sympathy from many people, especially African leaders, in appreciation of his considerable support for educational work in their country.

biography than simply some possible reflected glory from his famous father-in-law. He himself, though not a medical man, played an important part in advancing the health of Edinburgh.

Alexander Bruce was a director and an important influence in the development of William Younger and Co., the noted brewers of Holyrood. In the early 1880s Younger's products were far from satisfactory and they were steadily losing trade. This was due to problems in their fermentation process. In 1884 the Tercentenary Celebrations of Edinburgh University took place, and among the large number of highly distinguished representatives of learned bodies from all over the world who attended

DR JOHN D. COMRIE

Dr John D. Comrie

From "The Edinburgh Medical Journal"

FOR long enough anyone seeking reliable information on a point of Scottish medical history would be referred to "Comrie", the abbreviation for his 2-volume *History of Scottish Medicine*, the standard work. It was originally published in 1927 for the Wellcome Historical Medical Museum in London, resulting from a meeting of the British Medical Association held in Edinburgh that year. It was indeed a most detailed and scholarly work. As the preface points out, hitherto there had been separate historical accounts of various university medical schools and hospitals, but no work dealing with Scottish medicine as a whole. "Comrie" met this need. It presents an inspiring story, copiously illustrated, and as regards Edinburgh all the "giants" of its own once famous medical school are here.

Dr John Dixon Comrie was born on February 23rd 1875 in Buchan and educated at George Watson's College and Edinburgh University, graduating first in Arts and Natural Philosophy and then in Medicine. He became very widely experienced, studying in Berlin and Vienna and holding a wide variety of posts in Edinburgh, Glasgow and London. He was a consultant physician in the First World War and author of several books on medicine. A distinguished Edinburgh surgeon wrote of him: "A splendid teacher, an able physician, but primarily interested in the literary aspects of medicine". He was appointed Edinburgh's first Lecturer in the History of Medicine in 1909, and he added to his knowledge of Scottish medicine that of most major countries of the world. His illustrated lectures in the subject which so predominantly inspired him were much in demand and proved a source of fascination that aroused keenness and enthusiasm in young students. He was a popular physician of kindly spirit and unruffled calm. Of tall, military-like bearing, with a bristling moustache, colleagues nick-named him "The Kaiser". He died on October 1st 1939. Although numbers of important books have appeared on the history of medicine, whether Scottish or other, "Comrie" still remains in a class of its own.

PROFESSOR PETER HUME BROWN

RESIDENCE in Morningside seems

Professor Peter Hume Brown
By courtesy of Department of Scottish History
University of Edinburgh

to have attracted many Historiographers Royal for Scotland, even until quite recent times. The man who enjoyed this honoured title in 1907 was Professor Peter Hume Brown, who died on November 30th 1918 at his home in the Braids district. At the turn of the century, many Scottish schoolchildren must have learned the history of their country from Professor Hume Brown's *History of Scotland for Schools*, well illustrated and easily read, while the more junior pupils gained their knowledge from a more introductory book by Dr H. W. Meikle, another Morningside resident and later Historiographer Royal, who published his contribution at Professor Hume Brown's suggestion.

Peter Hume Brown was born at Tranent on December 17th 1849 and was educated at Prestonpans Free Church School, where he remained until the age of 20, acting as a pupil teacher. His father and mother died relatively young and he was brought up by somewhat discouraging relations. Upon leaving school he taught in Wales and Newcastle-upon-Tyne, then entered Edinburgh University as a student for the ministry. This aim he abandoned in 1874 and sought tutorial work abroad, but poor health spoiled his plans and he returned to graduate at Edinburgh University in 1875. He recorded his special appreciation of the distinguished Professor David Masson's influence on his studies and that of the works of Goethe and Saint-Beare. After graduation Hume Brown opened a private school in Edinburgh but closed this down after the untimely death of his wife and concentrated on history and literature research. His success in this latter field was meagre.

Two biographies, one on George Buchanan and the other, a theological study on John Knox, earned high praise. In 1899 Hume Brown published his *History of Scotland* and two years later was appointed Professor of Ancient History at Edinburgh University. Several scholarly books and essays followed on Scottish History, especially on the harsh terms for Scotland in the Act of Union with England; and a life of Goethe which he considered his greatest work. But he died before its publication, which was effected posthumously. Considered too careful and "safe" a writer, although a much more speculative talker, Professor Peter Hume Brown, after a rather varied career, earned a place among the most notable of Scottish historians.

In some of his writing he acknowledged the personal assistance of Mr Theodore Napier, the ardent Jacobite of the Merchiston district.

GEORG LICHTENSTEIN

MANY visitors to Morningside Cemetery must be rather surprised to encounter at its western end the grave of a former Hungarian patriot and musician once well known in Edinburgh, and may wonder why he rests here. Georg Lichtenstein was born in Hungary in about 1823. During the Austrian invasion of his country in 1850, as the Secretary to Louis Kossuth, the great Hungarian patriot who was murdered, Lichtenstein was eventually forced to go into exile. Travelling *via* Berlin he arrived

Grave of Georg Lichtenstein in Morningside Cemetery

Photograph by Mr P. Wark

in London in 1851 and, being a pianist and composer, began teaching music there. In 1855 he came to Edinburgh, where he soon acquired many pupils and gave many more concerts and recitals, notably at the old Theatre Royal and the Hopetoun Rooms. He was one of the founder members of the Edinburgh Society of Musicians and for a time was its President. His two nieces were also professional musicians in Edinburgh. He died on February 13th 1893. On his grave-stone are the inscriptions: "Professor of Music-Honorary Citizen of Edinburgh", and a line from a Hungarian patriotic anthem, "Be faithful to your country unto death".

SIR EDWARD APPLETON

OF the very many people of academic background and distinction interred in Morningside Cemetery, undoubtedly the most widely famous was Sir Edward Appleton. He has been described as one of the leading scientists of his generation and a research worker of the highest standing. Indeed, when he performed the opening ceremony at Napier College in 1964 this seemed most fitting, since if any living scientist was worthy to be associated with John Napier, a mathematician of truly world renown, it was Sir Edward Appleton.

Sir Edward, who died on April 21st 1965, pursued what were virtually three separate careers. Firstly, he was a research worker, who accomplished brilliant work at Cambridge on the ionosphere, on which he published nearly a hundred papers over 36 years. His discoveries led to

Sir Edward Appleton

In the robes of the Principal of Edinburgh University
Portrait by Sir William Hutchison
By kind permission of the University of Edinburgh

the naming of the "Appleton Layer". Later research involving the use of rockets and satellites only confirmed the accuracy of Sir Edward's earlier conclusions, which required no revision. For this work he was eventually awarded the Nobel Prize in Physics in 1947. Secondly, during the difficult Second World War years he had headed the Government's important Department of Scientific and Industrial Research. He was among the group of scientists who advised the Cabinet that the manufacture of the atomic bomb was possible and in 1943 be visited the United States to arrange collaboration between American and British scientists on the undertaking. Thirdly, Sir Edward, in 1949, resumed his career in the academic world when he became Principal and Vice-Chancellor of Edinburgh University, which post he held for 16

years until his death. Even his administrative duties as Principal did not diminish Sir Edward's enthusiasm for research and he continued to correspond with leading physicists.

A special University Court minute after his death included the words: "Throughout his busy life, without in any degree losing that human touch and capacity for enjoyment which so endeared him to all his friends, he maintained a feeling for the importance and dignity of the University rather than of himself, and never for one moment lost sight of the fact that he held a position of the most sacred trust".

The Principal, while never belittling the dignity of his high office, was remembered by all levels of staff, not least the manual workers, servitors and cleaners, for his "human touch". Sir Edward Appleton married Jessie Longston, daughter of a Huddersfield clergyman, and they had two daughters. His wife was one of the first women fabric designers in Britain. She died in 1964. In 1965 Sir Edward married Mrs Helen Allison, his secretary for 13 years, but he died suddenly at his home only a month after his marriage. One obituary of Sir Edward runs to 15 pages, while the list of his world-wide honours and scientific papers occupies an appendix of 6 pages.

DR DOUGLAS STRACHAN

TOURISTS in Europe are occasionally amazed, or quite simply incredulous, when shown the place of birth, studio, or university building, where some world-famous artist,

Dr Douglas Strachan

By courtesy of his daughter, Mrs Una Wallace

Balcarres Street you come upon the building close up, and then, if not already aware of the fact, marvel to think that here in this rather unlikely looking "studio" for nearly 20 years there worked a man described as "One of the greatest British stained glass artists of modern times". This was Dr Douglas Strachan, noted — not only in Britain but far beyond — for his own virtually unique ability in his chosen medium and also for creating a renewed interest in stained glass in Scotland and stimulating its emergence "from a long period of dull and pedestrian design and workmanship of products simply provided 'off the shelf'". Dr Strachan was to inspire a whole generation of young artists in stained glass.

Born in Aberdeen in 1875, educated at Robert Gordon's College, and then developing his artistic ability at Royal Scottish Academy "Life Schools", Douglas Strachan worked for some time as a lithographic artist on the Aberdeen Free Press and as a "black and white artist" on newspapers in Manchester and elsewhere. He further pursued his studies in London, France, Spain and Italy, and showed early promise as a portrait and figure painter. In 1908 he became Principal of the Design Department at the Edinburgh College of Art, but found this post too limited in scope. His distinguished career as a stained glass artist — largely self-taught — began with his being awarded the commission to produce four stained-glass windows for the Palace of Peace at The Hague, the United Kingdom's contribution to the décor of the famous building. To list Strachan's

writer or scholar was brought up, produced his work, taught or was taught, because it seems the most umpromising material environment and hardly conducive to the making of a genius. Without chromium-plated furnishings, spacious class-rooms, formica-covered benches or well-planned lighting, it seems nothing but the artist's innate ability and intuitive potential called forth the motivation, the indefinable creative drive, oblivious of surroundings. Such a thought may strike one as one turns into Balcarres Street, at Morningside Station, and sees almost immediately ahead of what was the former main entrance to the cemetery a far-from-elegant two-storey rectangular building made of brick. Entering through a pend or close between Nos 4 and 5 truly prodigious works all over Britain and overseas would be impossible within this short biography and his achievements have been catalogued elsewhere. Towards the end of his career and until his sudden death in 1950 he just could not cope with the commissions offered to him, although with characteristic dedication and consideration for others, he sought to meet his commitments, deeply regretting having to disappoint innumerable patrons.

Douglas Strachan's prominence during the periods following both World Wars led to an almost unlimited demand for memorials in stained glass. Among so many creations which might be regarded as his most notable works, his many obituary tributes agreed in singling out the Scottish National War Memorial — "The Shrine" — at the peak of Edinburgh Castle rock, the stained-glass windows of which were entirely his. These have been praised for their realism and modernity, the absence of conventional symbolism, and their factual (often stark) visual record of episodes in the First World War. The studied effect of the transmitted light is something to be experienced and that cannot be conveyed by mere words. All the artist's innate mysticism, all the subtlety of inspiration prompted by true depth of feeling can be sensed there: indeed, a fitting contribution to the over-all genius of The Shrine's architecture, the work of Sir Robert Lorimer.

Strachan himself apparently derived special personal satisfaction from the nine large windows he designed in 1933, constituting four years' work, for the parish church of St Thomas at Winchelsea in Sussex as a First World War Memorial to the Men of the Cinque Ports and the ancient towns of Rye and Winchelsea. One of the windows commemorates the deaths of the whole crew of the Rye harbour lifeboat *Mary Stanford* in an attempt to save a foreign ship. Much other work was carried out in England; but some of his best creative art may be seen in Edinburgh, Glasgow, and Aberdeen where, for example, his portrayal in glass of "Ancient and Modern Labour" for Aberdeen Trades Council is a striking expression of the artist's own personal interests as well as of his amazing versatility. In Glasgow University Chapel two 30-foot-high windows illustrate Glasgow's history from the ancient days of St Mungo to the modern Glasgow Fair. In Edinburgh's New College Library, too, some of Strachan's work may be seen.

Douglas Strachan, who had been elected as Honorary Member of the R.S.A. in 1920, was made an Honorary Doctor of Laws by Aberdeen University in 1923.

While still using the premises off Balcarres Street, in 1925, Dr Strachan was visited there by Queen Mary who was shown over his studio and the work he was engaged upon. In 1929, after the artist had moved from Balcarres Street and set up his studio within the precincts of his very fine villa "Pittendriech" at Lasswade, he was honoured by further royal visits. His home at Lasswade, where he died in 1950, housed a most valuable collection of Chinese works of art.

COUNCILLOR GEORGE HORNE

Councillor George Martin Horne

By courtesy of the City of Edinburgh District Council and with the kind assistance of Mr Charles Allan, City Officer, Mr Brian McGuire and Mr Rudi Ganarin

Photograph by Drummond Young

NO living recollection of the Morningside district of the late 1930s, and extending over a period of nearly twenty years, would be complete without reference to the man who earned for himself the title of "The Bishop of Blackford Hill". This was George Martin Horne, an evangelical lay missionary, whose premises were in the one-time Mission Hall at 10 Balcarres Street. Services were regularly conducted here by Mr Horne, who also on occasion spoke at street corners in the district. He also did much house-visiting and many Morningside families and individuals who were not his supporters nevertheless were the recipients of his generosity when in difficulties and his advice and supportive friendship. Mr Horne will be remembered best by many people for his Sunday afternoon services held on the grassy natural amphi-theatre at the top of the wooden steps leading up from Blackford Pond. Music was provided by a portable harmonium and a number of individual instrumentalists.

George Horne was elected to represent South Leith on Edinburgh Town Council in November 1935 and again from May 1949 until May 1959. He was convenor of the Cleansing and Lighting Sub-committee of the Streets and Buildings Committee from November 1938 to 1941 and a member of other committees, in all serving on the Council for nearly 20 years. He was still a member when he died in May 1959, and was buried in Morningside Cemetery.

TOMMY ARMOUR

IN a district such as Morningside, which tends perhaps to be rather heavily weighted historically on the side of the "landed gentry" and those distinguished in the academic world, in medicine, in literature, or other subjects through which they made "a valuable contribution towards society", it adds the spice of variety to present a former resident whose fame was gained in a very different field — on the golf course! This was one of the world's most successful sportsmen of modern times, Tommy Armour.

In the early 1900s a heavy partition of wooden railway sleepers extended across what is now Balcarres Street, at a point a little westward of the present-day entrance to Morningside Recreation Park. Beyond was a

Tommy Armour

By courtesy of "The Scotsman" Publications Ltd.

further area of the Plewlands estate stretching to the lower slopes of Easter Craiglockhart Hill or the lands of Craighouse. Here was a short 9-hole rather rough and ready golf course. Because his father was employed on the Craighouse hospital staff, young Tommy Armour was permitted to play. And play he did! The account which follows has all the features of a classical success story. By the age of 14 Tommy Armour, playing regularly over the Braid Hills course, was already a highly valued member of the Edinburgh Western Golf Club. There were then no boys' golf championship competitions, as such, but if there had been, it is said, Tommy Armour would undoubtedly have won them. While still in his teens he and his brother Sandy were in the Western's "Dispatch Trophy" team.

The outbreak of the First World War found Tommy exchanging his golfing gear for a private's uniform in the Tank Corps. When he was demobbed he had reached the rank of Major, but he had also been wounded, gassed, had metal plates inserted in his head and left arm and, most serious of all for a golfer, blinded in the left eye. But an indomitable spirit was one of Tommy Armour's main characteristics and, incredibly, he returned to the golf course. Before long, his old skill had returned, and soon his name was regularly in the sports page headlines. In 1920 he won the French Open Championship. In 1921 he was in the British amateur team playing against the United States, and then, after he had gone to settle in America, in 1926, came a unique distinction: he was in the USA professional team competing against Great Britain. Before long another unprecedented achievement: he won the British Open Championship, the United States Open and the P.G.A. Championship. On the way to achieving all these successes he had at last mastered his one long-standing weakness — he had been a poor putter! So much so that on one occasion earlier in his career, after his defeat in a Fife tournament, on his way home by train, he threw all his putters over the Forth Bridge into the deep waters below!

With such a reputation in world golf Tommy Armour might well have freely chosen on which American course to settle down as a professional coach. He took up an appointment at the Boca Racton Club just outside New York, where he was "pro" for 20 years. This club was the Mecca for innumerable rich

253

Americans. Its professional was not only a championship-class player, he was also a first-rate tutor. It was said that many an American business magnate would have sold a steel mill or a railroad or a few oil wells to pay Tommy to bring his handicap down. In the American golfing world the boy from Morningside, tall, lean, determined, yet with an irrepressible gaiety and humour, even under the strain of a championship contest, became a legend. Golf writers have contrasted his easy manner and showmanship with the tight-lipped seriousness of today's contestants. With his tuition fee of 100 dollars an hour readily paid by millionaire businessmen, film stars, (even ex-President Richard Nixon was once his pupil), Armour was reputedly a "two-million-dollar man". His golfing books, one in particular which reached ten editions in six languages, "written" by dictation over four days to a typist with experience of the game, made him a fortune, entering the American best-selling book list for fourteen weeks.

In August 1963 the late Frank Moran, celebrated golf correspondent of *The Scotsman*, as a tribute to his 50 years' service as such, had a trophy named after him "to be awarded annually to a Scot or person of Scots ancestry who has done most for golf. . . ." The first recipient was Tommy Armour.

Scotland's greatest-ever golfing ambassador became an American citizen. His son, Tommy D. Armour, a surgeon, had a distinguished career in the United States Army and won several commendation medals. Tommy Armour, senior, died in 1968, aged 72. Despite his appearing to "live, speak and dream golf", he never lost his sense of proportion. He once said: "It's nice to be a good golfer and win championships, but, Hell!, being the finest golfer in the world never cured anyone of polio". The Morningside exile's grandson, "Tommy Armour III", was amongst the participants in the British Open Championship at Turnberry in Ayrshire in July 1986.

DR ROBERT MOREHEAD

Dr Robert Morehead

From "*Memorials of the Life and Writings of the Rev. Robert Morehead, D.D.*", ed. Charles Morehead

PLEWLANDS FARM, formerly reached by a pathway which began just across what has been called the Comiston Burn, near the south end of the railway footbridge at Balcarres Street, from its outline in the early maps seems to have been quite extensive and its farm-house and other associated buildings rather substantial. Robert Cochrane in his *Pentland Walks* quotes from the diary of the Reverend Robert Morehead, one-time Episcopal Dean of Edinburgh, who was living at Plewlands Farm in 1823: "A most beautiful summer residence near Braid, where I am alone with my daughter Isabella. In the mornings I study Hebrew. I sometimes think of writing my journal here in blank verse. There is a great deal of poetry scattered about me if I could catch it".

The reference to Plewlands is from *Memories of the Life and Writings of the Reverend R. Morehead, D.D.*, published by his son, Dr Charles Morehead, M.D., F.R.C.P. (Ed) in 1875. This book provides a most detailed account of his father's life, including his many activities in Edinburgh as a churchman and educationalist. Dr Robert Morehead was born near Stirling on March 9th 1777. In his youth he resided in various parts of Scotland before going to England. He recalls that during his early years in Ayrshire, he met a Miss Wilhelmina Alexander, Robert Burns's "Bonnie Lass of Ballochmyle". He was also a friend of Thomas Campbell, the Scottish poet, who was a frequent guest at "Woodville" in Canaan Lane. After his ordination, he served as a curate in the Episcopalian church in the Cowgate (which later became St Patrick's Roman Catholic Church). He was appointed Episcopal Dean of Edinburgh in 1878.

In 1829 Dr Morehead and his wife and family were residing in a small villa at Corstorphine. In his journal he notes that his wife had observed that "the girls of the village were rough and neglected and neither taught morals, nor manners, nor sewing and knitting". With financial assistance from friends Dr Morehead and a group of people opened a school for girls, with a specially appointed school-mistress. Later, another similar school was opened at Craigcrook. Dr Morehead left for England some years later. His son Charles, who was born in Edinburgh, had quite a notable medical career and for some time was Principal of Grant Medical College, Bombay.

DR JOSEPH BELL

Dr Joseph Bell

JOSEPH BELL is best known, perhaps, as Conan Doyle's prototype for his famous character Sherlock Holmes. The famous novelist earlier in his life as a medical student in Edinburgh was taught by Bell and was so impressed — as were very many others — by the surgeon's acute powers of observation and deduction in his diagnosis of cases that he modelled Holmes on his old teacher. Dr Joseph Bell, like so many others, would seem to be remembered now in the context of reflected glory, in his case of Doyle's creation. Yet he was, in fact, quite distinguished in his own right, as a most competent surgeon, and added his lustre to that of the Edinburgh medical school of his day.

Joseph Bell was born in 1837 and educated at Edinburgh Academy, beginning his medical studies at the age of 16. He was the great-grandson of the famous Edinburgh surgeon Dr Benjamin Bell, who also developed the lands of Newington. For some time he was one of Professor James Styme's "bright boys" in his Royal Infirmary surgical team. Dr Joseph Bell, having completed fifteen years' service with Syme, under "the 15-year rule" had to resign his Infirmary post. This was most timely for the managers of the Royal Hospital for Sick Children, Edinburgh's first such hospital, which had opened in Lauriston Lane in 1860 and then moved to larger premises in Meadowside House on the site where the Simpson Memorial Maternity Pavilion was eventually built. In 1887, when Joseph Bell, aged 49, left the Royal Infirmary, he accepted a post as surgeon to the Hospital for Sick Children, then on the north side of the Meadows. He was also then beginning his three year period as President of the Royal College of Surgeons of Edinburgh. He was indeed a very notable surgeon of high reputation and very much in demand.

In 1890 an outbreak of typhoid fever in the Meadowside House Hospital, which entailed several

Dr Joseph Bell

Leaving his home in Edinburgh's Melville Crescent on daily visit to Royal Hospital for Sick Children at Plewlands. From "The Medical School of Edinburgh" by Dr Douglas Guthrie

fatalities, emphasised the need for a much larger children's hospital. Consequently it was decided to build a new one, designed by George Washington Browne, at a cost of £40,000, in Sciennes Road, and this opened in 1895. While it was being built the children and staff from Meadowside House were moved temporarily to a very large building which stood on the Plewlands estate at the corner of what is now Morningside Drive and Morningside Grove. It had been built in about 1882 as Morningside Hydropathic but seems never to have really functioned as such for long, if at all, and within a short time became Morningside College, an expensive private school for boys. In 1889 the college transferred to "Rockville", the house built by James Gowans in Napier Road in 1858, and then eventually to the vacated Falcon Hall. The very commodious building conveniently available at Morningside Drive was re-named Plewlands House and here the Royal Hospital for Sick Children existed from 1890 to 1895.

The temporary children's hospital was rather far out from the city for the treatment of out-patients and the daily attendance of medical students, and Meadowside House remained open to serve these purposes. However, Dr Joseph Bell was driven out to Plewlands House daily in his horse-drawn Victorian carriage from his home in Melville Crescent. Bell, apart from his acute powers of observation and deduction in diagnosis, which had so impressed Conan Doyle, was also a very popular and successful teacher. He was a great admirer of Florence Nightingale and dedicated his important book *Notes on Surgery for Nurses* to her.

Indeed, the training of nurses was one of his important contributions to the development of medical treatment and he was the mainspring of the Queen Victoria Jubilee Institute for Nurses until his death. His other great interest was in children who were ill and he was ernestly dedicated to them. His published papers and other notes reveal how scholarly and advanced was his knowledge of the wide variety of children's diseases then encountered in the hospital, and he made some early observations on antibiotic phenomena which he observed so long before Sir Alexander Fleming's discovery of penicillin.

Dr Joseph Bell retired in 1897, spending much time at his pleasant house in the Mauricewood Road just beyond Flotterstone. In his younger days he was a keen cricketer and still remained an interested spectator. He was the last of the alternation of Benjamins and Josephs Bell who had all been surgeons in Edinburgh, his only son having died on military service when young. Dr Joseph Bell died in 1911. Much renewed interest in one of Edinburgh's great surgeons and in his association with Conan Doyle has arisen through a recent publication by Owen Dudley Edwards and an American author, Dr Ely M. Liebow, of North-Eastern Illinois University, in the very detailed biography: *Dr Joe Bell: Model for Sherlock Holmes.*

8 · CRAIGHOUSE/ CRAIGLOCKHART

SIR THOMAS CLOUSTON

Dr Thomas Clouston

From illustrated complimentary retiral dinner menu
Photograph by king permission of the Royal Edinburgh Hospital

THE successive medical or physician superintendents of what for long was known as the Royal Edinburgh Asylum, now the Royal Edinburgh Hospital, during their periods of office, each tended to represent and introduce a new era and developments, often including the building of new premises. This is expressed in the naming of two large and important sections of the hospital. One was McKinnon House, formerly the Western Department or West House, entered from Morningside Terrace or at the rear, from Tipperlinn Road, and in 1967 renamed in tribute to Dr William McKinnon, the first Physician Superintendent, appointed when the new building was completed and who initiated new approaches in administration, organisation and treatment. The other was The Thomas Clouston Clinic at Craighouse, so named in 1972 to commemorate the Physician Superintendent responsible for the building of this great new addition to the Royal Edinburgh Asylum in 1894 and, in his turn, introducing a new era into the understanding and treatment of mental illness.

Thomas Smith Clouston was born in Orkney in 1840, and was always proud of his Norse descent. Educated at Aberdeen Grammar School, he entered Edinburgh University Medical School where he was a constant prize winner. There he was greatly influenced by three of his teachers: Professor James Syme, Professor James Y. Simpson and Professor Laycock, the last-named including psychiatry in his lectures on general medicine. Following a short period demonstrating in anatomy, and after gaining his Doctorate in Medicine, Clouston was appointed an assistant to Dr Skae at the Royal Edinburgh Asylum. After two years, and at the early age of 23, he was appointed Superintendent of Cumberland and Westmorland Asylum, Carlisle, where he remained for ten years, carrying out much clinical research. On Dr Skae's death in 1873 Thomas Clouston succeeded

258

him as Physician Superintendent at Edinburgh.

There were two main features developing in the treatment of mental disorders. Dr Skae had sought to introduce much more detailed classification of various conditions — not always readily agreed upon by younger colleagues. He had also extended the teaching of psychiatry in the Medical School curriculum. Dr Thomas Clouston, in succeeding him, further developed both these approaches, especially the teaching element and, in 1879, he was the first lecturer appointed in psychiatry at Edinburgh University, an historic step. The teaching of the subject in its own right and no longer as an appendage to general medicine was begun, culminating in the establishment of the first Chair in the subject in 1918, with Professor George Robertson as the incumbent.

Soon after his appointment as Physician Superintendent of the Asylum Dr Clouston began pressing for additional accommodation. In Dr McKinnon's time there had been 88 patients and in Dr Skae's, 466, due to new legislation and local authority responsibilities. Advancement in knowledge and new forms of treatment meant more admissions. Dr Clouston no doubt had often gazed from the overcrowded McKinnon House westwards towards the not-too-distant pleasant and spacious lands of Craighouse and envisaged building there. His dream materialised. In 1878 he persuaded the Asylum managers to purchase the Craighouse estate, including the 16th-century mansion-house of Old Craig. Clouston tempered his delight at the new prospects with realism, not immediately proceeding to build but first visiting Europe and the USA to study mental hospitals there. He eventually decided upon the Scottish baronial mansion style which was to become one of the city's great and impressive landmarks. With the assistance of an architect-patient and the professional services of Sydney Mitchell, the plans were drawn, which included the vast hospital building and, as a feature of deliberate policy, the various pleasant villas to be used for certain types of patients. The new hospital was intended for private, and often quite wealthy, patients who paid fairly substantial fees and in the administrative block was built the Grand Hall, of magnificent design and atmosphere with its minstrels' gallery and great fire-places, the setting for dinners, concerts, musical recitals and early film shows.

Part of Dr Clouston's motivation in providing only the best facilities he often expressed thus: "We can never do too much for our patients to make up for the cruelty of past ages". Again: "The plan is brightness and light. Everywhere maximum light and cheerful colours. Truly the light is sweet". And again: "The arrangements required for the worst class of patient should never be used for the best. Cure, not mere confinement, should be the keynote of our approach". The foundation stone was laid on July 16th 1890 by the 10th Earl of Stair, Deputy Governor of the new hospital, and the opening ceremony was performed by the Duke of Buccleuch, Governor, on October 26th 1894. The cost of the new building and villas was £150,000. Details remain of the strict régime which Dr Clouston enforced — the utmost care and consideration for all patients — but meticulous regulations to ensure their safety. There were notices, many of which remain in the archives, which read: "Anyone leaving this door open will be fined sixpence" (Sgd) T. S. Clouston, M.S. "Nurses are not permitted to marry without prior consultation with the hospital authorities."

Dr Thomas Clouston retired in 1908 after thirty-five years' service as Physician Superintendent. The signed menu of his special and select Presentation Dinner is also among the hospital archives which with many other items will form the basis of a historical museum. Dr Clouston was knighted in 1911. In his profession his clinical skill was considered brilliant and his contribution to psychiatry outstanding and of world repute, including his researches into the scientific and laboratory aspects of the subject. He was a first-class administrator, a vivid, fascinating lecturer, and author of several important text-books. He was awarded honorary LL.D. degrees by the Universities of Edinburgh and Aberdeen and was widely respected in the social life of Edinburgh. His elder son J. Storer Clouston was a well-known novelist and writer. Sir Thomas Clouston died in 1915.

DR JOHN HILL BURTON

WHILE Dr Thomas Clouston may have been rejoicing in 1878 that the managers of the Royal Edinburgh Asylum had acquired the lands of Craighouse, including the 16th-century mansion-house, and were

Dr John Hill Burton
by W. B. Hole
From Burton's "The Book Hunter"

soon to erect on the hill a magnificent large new building for private fee-paying patients, there was another man who, while perhaps appreciating the importance of the new development, nevertheless experienced the deepest personal disappointment. This was Dr John Hill Burton, and his feelings arose from the fact that he had been the tenant of the old Craighouse 16th-century mansion-house for nearly seventeen years, and it had become his family home, set in such a magnificent situation and so conducive to his work as an author. Furthermore, the notice given to him by the asylum managers that he must vacate the mansion had been very short. Fortunately, coincidental with the need for Dr Hill Burton and his family to leave Craighouse, the fine villa, Morton House, the dower house of the Trotters of nearby

Mortonhall and situated in the secluded district of Winton, off what is now Frogston Road West, had become vacant, and the Burton family acquired its lease. There Dr Hill Burton resided until his death in the house on August 10th 1881.

Born in Aberdeen, John Hill Burton won a bursary from the Grammar School to Marischal College, where he graduated principally in law. He was called to the Scottish Bar in 1831. He seems to have preferred authorship and the study of history to legal practice and earned a considerable livelihood from his books and articles for nearly half a century. His work ranged widely: law, politics, theology, history, geology, botany, biography and bibliography. His major books were: *A History of Scotland* in 8 volumes; *A Manual of the Law of Scotland* and *A Life of David Hume*. He was an outdoor enthusiast, enjoying walking and camping. Frequently he covered thirty miles a day on foot. One of his many articles for *Blackwood's Magazine* included "Hints for an Autumnal Ramble". Having written widely and deeply on so many subjects, Hill Burton always felt rather insulted that his book *The Bookhunter*, written as entertainment, received such great praise compared with his other works. He was appointed Historiographer Royal for Scotland in 1867 and was considered second only to David Laing as an antiquarian and for his knowledge of early Scottish life.

Dr Hill Burton married somewhat late in life and previously had lived in many parts of Edinburgh. Characteristically, perhaps, as an historian and antiquarian, he preferred the Old Town to Edinburgh's elegant New Town across the North Bridge. His wife, Isabella Lauder, whom he married in 1844, died five years later, leaving him with three infant daughters. In August 1855 he married Katharine Innes, daughter of his close friend, the distinguished Scottish historian Dr Cosmo Innes, and after residing for some years in the city, in March 1861 he enters the South Edinburgh chronicles as having presented to his wife an unusual birthday present — the keys to the old 16th-century mansion-house at Craighouse, which his wife had known and loved since her childhood, and in which she had always longed to live. This was to become, with all its ancient historical associations and legends, their most pleasant family home.

In 1845 Dr Hill Burton had been appointed Secretary of the Prison Board at a salary of £700 per annum. From Craighouse, he walked daily to and from the Board's Offices in George Street. He became a well-known, eccentric figure to the people of Morningside, as he passed by in his long, black, shapeless coat, its large pockets stuffed with books and newspapers. One biographer wrote of his appearance: "... his black coat cut by the tailor without any very close acquaintance with the angularities of the form it was to cover. He was a fine, manly, independent, sincere, honest soul that was lodged in this somewhat shabby tabernacle". And at Craighouse "it was books, books, books everywhere". Dr Hill Burton's library there was estimated at 10,000 volumes and it was said he could find any book almost immediately even in darkness. A corner of his library is among the engravings by his daughter in *The Bookhunter*, which also contains a quite lengthy biographical introduction by Burton's second wife, Katharine.

Burton had four more children by his second marriage, and the family pony and trap used for conveying his family to and from the city was a familiar sight in Morningside. He preferred to isolate himself from visitors to Craighouse but did welcome Captain N. Speke, author of *The Discovery of the Source of the Nile*, who appreciated the experienced author's advice on the setting out of his book. "Yellow-haired wee Willie Burton", as Morningside people referred to him, was Burton's youngest son and became an engineer and it is said that during some time he spent in Japan he passed on much technical skill to some of their industries.

Dr John Hill Burton received many honours, including honorary LL.D. degrees from Aberdeen and Edinburgh Universities and a D.C.L. from Oxford, and was elected a member of the Athenaeum Club in London. In early 1877 he received the request to vacate Craighouse by Whitsun of that year. The lease he obtained of Morton House was most timely. During his family's removal to this slightly smaller house Dr Burton sold most of his vast library. By January 1881 his deteriorating health had become critical and he became confined to bed. During his last days the Reverend Belcome of Christ Episcopal Church at Holy Corner was a frequent and welcome visitor. Dr Burton apparently insisted on writing to the end and was still doing so, propped up in bed surrounded by his beloved books, when he died on August 10th 1881.

At his own request he was buried not in the Dean Cemetery, resting-place of so many prominent Edinburgh authors and artists, but in Dalmeny Churchyard beside one of his little daughters who had died in childhood.

CRAIGLOCKHART

THE great Scottish baronial building of the Thomas Clouston Clinic clings to the slopes of Easter Craiglockhart Hill, often simply referred to as Craighouse Hill. Across the Merchants of Edinburgh golf course and under the crest of Wester Craig-lockhart Hill stands the rather different Italianate former Craig-lockhart Hydropathic. Formerly, since 1920, the Convent of the Sacred Heart and from more recent times St Andrew's College of Education, it has now been sold by its Roman Catholic owners to Napier College. Whatever may result from the purchase of the building and its site, it is to be hoped that, externally at least, some semblance of the original hydropathic will remain and this not only to preserve a well-known and, visually, an almost indispensable land-mark on the city's skyline but also to retain some tangible reminder of one memorable era in the history of the building which is part of Edinburgh's (and indeed the nation's) literary heritage: the residence here and first meeting of the famous First World War poets Siegfried Sassoon and Wilfred Owen. But there are other names which must feature in the early chronicles of Craiglockhart.

THE MONRO DYNASTY

The Monro Dynasty

From *"The Story of a Great Hospital"* by A. Logan Turner
Portraits 1, 2 and 4 reproduced by kind permission of the Royal College of Surgeons, Edinburgh. Portrait 3 is in a private collection

THIS was one of the important sagas in the history of Edinburgh's Medical School. Professor Alexander Monro, *primus*, Professor of Anatomy from 1720 and virtually the founder of the Medical School proper, and certainly responsible for the beginning of its world-wide reputation, was succeeded by his son in the Chair, Alexander Monro, *secundus*, who in reputation equalled his father and in certain respects was destined even to outshine him. The third Monro was Alexander, *tertius*, who also acquired the Chair, in 1798, but whatever his redeeming qualities may have been in other respects they were not in the teaching or practice of anatomy. In 1773 Alexander Monro, *secundus*, having acquired considerable income from the fees paid by the very large number of students who attended his anatomy lectures, purchased the estate of Craiglockhart. While he never resided there, but at St Andrew Square, he took a keen interest in his new estate and extensively developed it. He built himself a comfortable little country house at Craiglockhart and there entertained liberally, the hospitality of his dinner parties becoming almost legendary. His son Alexander, *tertius*, was encountering increasing criticism of his ability as Professor of Anatomy, and eventually such a point was reached due to vigorous and vociferous student protests and staff complaints that, to the University Court's great relief, he resigned in 1846, ending the 26-year-long "Monro Dynasty". His father, as mentioned, had bought Craiglockhart though not resided there; Alexander *tertius* found the district, still remote from the city, a welcome retreat after his stormy years in the Medical School. He built for himself the 22-roomed Craiglockhart House, which still stands, originally described as "sweetly situated on the verge of the sloping wooded bank which runs down to the Water of Leith". It may be seen today in Craiglockhart Dell Road, in much reduced grounds and surrounded by bungalows. Here resided Monro, *tertius*, with his large family. One of his sons, David, perpetuated the name of Craiglockhart in far-off regions. When he emigrated to New Zealand he named two of his properties there "Craiglockhart".

JAMES BELL

IN 1873 much of the land to the west had been acquired by the Craiglockhart Estate Company and four years later, this company feued thirteen acres to the Craiglockhart Hydropathic Company which erected what has been described as a "giant Italian villa", certainly a fitting description interiorly and exteriorly with its extensive and impressive parquet-floor main corridor with arched bays and large rooms leading off. The chairman of the Hydropathic Company was Mr Robert Hutchinson and the director when the hydro first opened was the resident physician, Dr Thomas D. Wilson, an Edinburgh general practitioner, since the main emphasis of the great new enterprise — in an era of such places — was on convalescence and health improvement. Gradually this aspect diminished and there was no longer a resident physician. A brochure setting out the establishment's attractions and lavish facilities for "hydropathy" is still extant, also a silk printed prospectus listing the daily and weekly time-table and the strict regulations.

From the beginning, however, Craiglockhart hydro seems to have encountered serious financial problems. Large loans were contracted and attempts made to sell, at a steadily reducing price. In 1890, the building was at last sold, for £12,500 — it had cost £46,000 — to Mr James Bell, the lessee of Dunblane Hydropathic. Bell was acting for a newly-established body, the Edinburgh Hydropathic Company, Ltd, of which he was secretary. Under his management and reduced terms the financial situation improved. After its use as a military hospital during the 1914-18 war, the hydro re-opened briefly. In

Mr James Bell
From "Edinburgh and the Lothians at the Opening of the 20th Century" by Alexander Eddington

1920 the company went into liquidation and the building and lands were sold to the Society of the Sacred Heart.

Little is on record concerning James Bell, who attempted to save the hydro from closure. He was a native of Thornhill, in Dumfriesshire, and after coming to Edinburgh became a Justice of the Peace for Midlothian. He was married to Eliza, daughter of John Duncan of Dundee. Whether the Morningside Hydropathic built at the top of Morningside Drive in about 1880 was also the property of the Edinburgh Hydropathic Company is difficult to ascertain. It would now appear that in fact the Morningside Hydropathic was never used as such and was sold soon after completion to the managers of Morningside College. Perhaps the company sought a more profitable venture at Craiglockhart.

264

SIEGFRIED SASSOON AND WILFRED OWEN

Siegfried Sassoon

DURING the First World War the health-restoring attractions of Craig-lockhart Hydropathic were with-drawn for some time while the building served a much more grim purpose, becoming a military hospital for officers suffering from shell-shock — sometimes considered a rather suspect condition — and other afflictions of stress and nervous disorders. It was to this hospital that the two famous war poets were sent, and where for the first time they met. Second-Lieutenant Siegfried Sassoon had, in fact, refused to serve further in a war which he considered unjust. On July 30th 1917 his case was raised in the House of Commons. A difficult issue: Sassoon was certainly no coward, having shown unusual courage and been awarded the Military Cross. He was regarded as having suffered a nervous breakdown, and arrived at Craiglockhart Military Hospital under the care of the noted psychiatrist Dr W. H. R. Rivers. Whatever the content of their clinical sessions, Sassoon the patient continued to write poetry and his feelings at Craiglockhart are perhaps best expressed in his poem "Sick Leave".

> When I'm asleep and dreaming and
> lulled and warm:
> They come, the homeless ones, the
> noiseless dead.
> While the dim charging breakers of the
> storm
> Bellow and drone and rumble
> overhead
>
> Out of the gloom, they gather about my
> bed.
> They whisper to my heart; their
> thoughts are mine:
> "Why are you here, with all your
> watches ended?
> From Ypres to Frise, we sought you in
> the line."
> In bitter safety I awake, unfriended;
> And, while the dawn begins with
> slashing rain,
> I think of the battalion in the mud.
> "When are you going out to them
> again?
> Are they not still your brothers
> through our blood?"

When Sassoon arrived at Craig-lockhart another young officer was already there, unknown to Sassoon, who was a genuine case of shell-shock and stress after many terrible ordeals at the front line — Wilfred Owen. He, too, while under treatment, was expressing his reactions in poetry. They met in August 1917 when Owen, plucking up courage and taking the first step, knocked on Sassoon's door and

Wilfred Owen

What passing bells for those who die as
  cattle?
Only the monstrous anger of the guns.
Only the stuttering rifle's rapid rattle
Can patter out their hasty orizons.
No mockeries for them; no prayers nor
  bells,
Nor any voice of mourning save the
  choirs —
The shrill demented choirs of wailing
  shells;
And bugles calling for them from sad
  shires.
What candles may be held to speed
  them all?
Not in the hands of boys but in their
  eyes
Shall shine the holy glimmers of
  goodbyes.
The pallor of girls' brows shall be their
  pall;
Their flowers the tenderness of patient
  minds,
And each slow dusk a drawing-down of
  blinds.

diffidently introduced himself; eventually he got around to mentioning his poetry. It was a meeting of very great importance for each of them and of inestimable value for our poetic heritage. Together they virtually took over the production of *The Hydra*, the hospital house magazine, and some of their best work first appeared in its unpretentious pages. One of Owen's works, believed to have been refined and completed with Sassoon's assistance, and first published in *The Hydra*, was his famous "Anthem for Doomed Youth". The final draft, on hospital notepaper, bearing Sassoon's pencilled corrections, still survives:

Their friendship at Craiglockhart was necessarily short-lived but it was precious to each and of great consequence. Apart from their shared sense of a mission against war through poetry, they were very different from each other. Sassoon was of the English country gentleman background, keen on hunting, cricket and golf, which he played at the Mortonhall Club's course while he was at Craiglockhart; on other occasions he frequented a number of Princes Street Clubs. An extrovert, Sassoon originally entered the war as "the happy warrior". Owen was of humbler social background, had taught in England and Bordeaux, was more serious and introspective. While at Craiglockhart he had taught briefly at Tynecastle School where he was long remembered. Sassoon

266

returned to the war, was wounded and survived. Later Owen also returned, quite near the war's end, and was killed at Oise-Sambre Canal a week before Armistice. A delayed telegram had tragically misled his parents into thinking he was safe.

Sassoon was to continue his writing, and won many literary awards. Owen, his life and literary career cut short, has nevertheless been considered by many as the foremost of the Great War poets. Over the years many people have been deeply interested and silently impressed to have seen the rooms in the former hospital where Sassoon and Owen resided while under treatment and the corridors in which they walked, each helping to shape the other's poetic creations. The BBC made an excellent video film some years ago of the poets at Craiglockhart. Very many people will hope that in any changes to come not all vestiges of this famous buildings' memorable past will disappear beyond recognition.

9 · GREENBANK/TOWARDS COMISTON

THE top of Easter Craiglockhart Hill above the Thomas Clouston Clinic is a good vantage-point from which to view much development further to the south. And in the forefront, just beyond Greenlea old people's home, in earliest days the City Poorhouse, is an extensive building whose establishment here at Greenbank in 1903 marked the end of one long-drawn-out era in the saga of Edinburgh's public health advancement and the beginning of another, most beneficial one. This is the City Hospital, originally the City Infectious Diseases Hospital, and the names of four people of the time will always be most closely associated with the inspiration behind its initiation, construction and eventual opening ceremony. They are four men all of different professions.

Dr Henry Duncan Littlejohn
by Sir George Reid
By courtesy of the National Galleries of Scotland, Edinburgh

DR HENRY LITTLEJOHN

THE establishment of a proper fever hospital was one of the major objectives of Dr Henry Littlejohn during the extremely long period of his distinguished services as the city's first Medical Officer of Health. The decision by the Town Council to appoint an M.O.H. was in itself a most important and significant advancement in the attitude of the civic authorities. Dr Henry Duncan Littlejohn was appointed to the newly created post in 1862, and three years later published his major report on the health and sanitary conditions of the city. In terms of to-day's vastly improved situation the picture presented in the Littlejohn Report must now seem an appalling one. In the grossly overcrowded and insanitary tenements of the Old Town, Dr Littlejohn reported that frequently "disease spreads like wild-fire". In 1867 the Public Health (Scotland) Act placed health among the responsibilities of the local authorities. Attempts to isolate and treat infectious cases were made first in the old Royal Infirmary in Infirmary Street and then in the new hospital at Lauriston, but such provisions were quite inadequate and medically unsound. In 1865, Dr Littlejohn estimated the number of infectious diseases cases in the city at any given time as never below six hundred. On every possible occasion the M.O.H. urged the opening of a

268

new and purpose-built infectious diseases hospital.

During Louis Pasteur's visit to Edinburgh in 1884 to attend the University's Tercentenary Celebrations he met Dr Littlejohn and others concerned to act following upon the whole new concept of infectious disease brought about by Pasteur's then relatively recent discovery of the nature of bacteria. One consequence of the discussions with Pasteur was the opening of the Usher Institute of Public Health in Warrender Park Road in 1902, through the generosity of Sir Thomas Usher and Alexander Bruce. This was the first great victory for Dr Littlejohn's campaigns, the new institute supplementing what he had already done for public health by advocating improved housing, the compulsory notification of infectious disease (which became law in 1879) and other social measures. A year later saw the next great and final landmark in Littlejohn's long career, with the opening in May 1903 of the City Infectious Diseases Hospital, or Colinton Hospital, as it was originally known, in Greenbank Drive.

Henry Duncan Littlejohn was born in Edinburgh in 1826 of long-established mercantile background. He was educated at Perth Academy and Edinburgh High School, of which he was *Dux*. Sometime after his graduation in Medicine, he initiated a course in Medical Jurisprudence in Edinburgh's Medical School in 1856, eventually occupying the Chair in this subject: this was long afterwards — in 1877, at the age of 51. In the 1880s his lectures in this subject were attracting an average attendance of 250 students. But Dr Littlejohn's special interest and almost passionate concern was public health, now termed community medicine. He was the natural choice as the city's first M.O.H. in 1862, and was as brilliant a teacher as ardent reformer, fascinating his students with his proposals and disturbing those in public life who were opposed to change. A devoutly religious man, he carried out much generous voluntary work in slum districts and was the ready champion and constant counsellor of poor people. Littlejohn was awarded an Honorary LL.D. by Edinburgh University in 1893 and knighted two years later. He was elected president of several medical societies and edited a number of medical journals. During his incredible length of service (of 50 years) as M.O.H. his influence on Edinburgh Town Council and its Public Health Committee was apparently quite amazing. He died on September 30th 1914, aged 88, eleven years after he had seen his dream of a "proper fever hospital" become a reality. His major obituary concluded with the words freely adapted from *Hamlet*: "Take him for all in all, we shall not look upon his like again".

BAILIE JAMES POLLARD

WHILE Dr Henry Littlejohn was the leader of many campaigns for reform in the city's housing and public health provision, it is true to say that in the Town Council he did have "friends in court". One of these in particular was Bailie James Pollard, who exercised much persuasion with those empowered to consider building the much-needed infectious diseases hospital. An orphan from a

Bailie James Pollard

and Copenhagen — and through the influence of Dr Littlejohn — Pollard became convinced that the new infectious diseases hospital should be built outwith the city. He published a booklet: *The Care of the Public Health and the New Fever Hospital in Edinburgh*, which is a most valuable source of information. Pollard certainly played a highly important part in the campaign.

ROBERT MORHAM

Robert Morham

By courtesy of Miss Margaret Buchanan

very poor social background in the city, James Pollard had obtained an apprenticeship with an Edinburgh accountancy firm and he gained admission to the Heriot-Watt College and subsequently qualified as an accountant in 1873. Pollard became an ardent member of the Fountainbridge Free Church, which eventually formed the congregation of the Barclay Free Church at Bruntsfield Links. He was also active in the Parliamentary Debating Society which met in Queen Street Hall in the 1880s and attracted huge audiences. He entered the Town Council in 1883, but when he was Chairman of the Public Health Committee in 1891 the vacated former Royal Infirmary in Infirmary Street had become the City's "fever hospital", and Pollard favoured the building of a new hospital but on the Infirmary Street site. However, after a study of similar hospitals in Basle, Zürich, Innsbrück, Vienna, Berlin, Hamburg

DURING Bailie Pollard's extensive tour of European cities prior to the Edinburgh authorities deciding upon the layout and facilities of the new hospital to be built at Greenbank, he was joined by the city architect of the time, Robert Morham, who eventually designed the buildings. Morham was born in Edinburgh on March 31st 1839 and was educated at

270

Newington Academy, the High School, and then studied at the Watt Institute and School of Art and the Board of Manufacturers' Art School. He received early training under David Rhind and David Bryce, both distinguished Edinburgh architects. After a short sojourn in London he returned to Edinburgh to become assistant to David Cousin, the City Architect or Superintendent of Works, and eventually succeeded him in office on his retiral in 1873. He completed much of the work which Cousin had initially designed.

As City Architect Morham was responsible for a great deal of public building in Edinburgh. This included the original Waverley Market, now a modern shopping complex, the meat market in Fountainbridge near the corner of Semple Street, public swimming baths at Dalry, Infirmary Street, Glenogle and Portobello, a number of public wash-houses, five district police stations, including the impressive building at the corner of Sciennes House Place and Causeway-side, and the central Fire Station at Lauriston. In addition he designed the bridge over the Water of Leith at Saughton Park, the prominent clock-towered Marchmont St Giles Church at the junction of Kilgraston Road and Grange Road, and some restoration of Gladstone's Land in the Lawnmarket. His largest undertaking was the City Infectious Diseases Hospital at Greenbank, begun in 1896 and opened in 1903. Robert Morham's sketch of the overall plan of the hospital with its symmetrical layout is fascinating in itself and a work of art, as are the sketch plans for certain groups and individual isolation wards. The deep red sandstone was chosen to convey a sense of warmth; the traditional type of peninsular wards, running north and south, ensured maximum sunlight from dawn to sunset, this of course with a keen appraisal of the therapeutic importance of sunlight very much in mind. Mr Morham, who latterly resided at 13 Lauder Road, died in 1912.

SIR JAMES STEEL

Lord Provost Sir James Steel
By courtesy of the City of Edinburgh Art Centre

THE association with the new hospital was for each a very practical matter; however, for long strongly campaigning for its provision and then executing its design and construction, there was a fourth public figure connected with it who, although much less active, was in the end more prominent in the public eye. This was the Lord Provost in office at the time of opening, Sir James Steel of Murieston, who presided over the official ceremony performed by King Edward VII.

James Steel, son of a farmer of Cambusnethan, was born in 1830 and after some years' residence in Wishaw came to Edinburgh in 1866, where he established a prosperous business as a builder and quarry-master. Steel built much of the city's Dalry area, the streets there named Murieston from his own title, also the fine terraced houses of Douglas, Glencairn and Eglinton Crescents at the West End. Belgrave Place, parts of Belgrave Crescent, and Buckingham Terrace were also his work. In 1894, purchasing land in Comely Bank from Colonel Learmonth, he built flats there and provided a bowling-green for the use of residents at a nominal fee.

Steel's building operations made him very wealthy, as one incident reveals. It is recorded that on one occasion, a tax official upon asking him his annual income was given the figure £80,000. When the official apologised, explaining that he was not seeking information as regards Steel's total assets but simply his annual income: the original figure was restated as the answer to this question. Steel was among the early members of the original Braid Church in Morningside — the little "iron kirk" at the foot of Braid Road, and he was a generous bene-factor of the congregation which eventually went to its new building at the corner of Nile Grove in 1887.

Entering the Town Council in 1872 and representing George Square ward for 31 years, undoubtedly Steel's "finest hour" was the part he played in the opening of the City Infectious Diseases Hospital on May

Lord Provost Sir James Steel

In civic robes (extreme left) with Edward VII (with plumed hat) at opening of City Fever Hospital, May 13th, 1903 by courtesy of the City Fever Hospital

13th, 1903. After the arrival at the main entrance of Edward VII and Queen Alexandra, with an escort of mounted Life Guards, the platform party outside the administrative block was assembled with great dignity and protocol. The special key for the official opening of the door was presented to the king. Some confusion appeared to arise at the doorway, both the Lord Provost and Edward VII attempting to go through the door together. Each gave way to the other, until at last, Steel in his characteristic "guid Scots tongue" was heard to say: "Hoots, man! we'll both gang in thegither!" Impasse or not, Steel was knighted after the ceremony. He died shortly after relinquishing the Lord Provost's office in September 1904. After his death, in the terms of his will, the Sir James Steel Trust was established. Originally, this was to provide very small sums of money annually, around £72, for men who had retired from the building industry, including tradesmen, with-out a pension. The Trust remains, along with the more ancient Trinity Hospital Fund, administered by Edinburgh District Council. Its future is in doubt and new applications for assistance are no longer considered.

TOWARDS COMISTON

As we retrace our steps from Greenbank and Craiglockhart to Comiston Road and are about to proceed finally now by Comiston to Swanston, the association of three notable people with the official opening of South Morningside Primary School in Comiston Road on October 3rd 1892 calls for some elaboration. The building of the school was completed by 1891 but the first pupils were not enrolled until September 5th 1892. The formal opening ceremony did not in fact take place until October 3rd 1892. The provision of this new primary school in what in the relatively short period between the early 1880s and 1892 had become a most populous suburb, seemed to be regarded as a very important event by the Education Authority, the St Cuthbert's and Dean School Board. This is signified by the presence and participation at the opening ceremony of two very distinguished gentlemen, Professor David Masson, the principal speaker, and none other than the famous philanthropist of legendary wealth Andrew Carnegie, who was accompanied by his wife. Both extolled the educational opportunities now afforded the children of Morningside and district — nearly 500 enrolments had taken place compared with under 100 pupils at the Old School-house which had just closed. A summary of the speeches can yet be found in the City Library Edinburgh Room files.

PROFESSOR DAVID MASSON

Professor David Masson

From "Quasi Cursores", Portraits of the High Officers and Professors of the University of Edinburgh at its Tercentenary, 1884

A VERY distinguished scholar, Masson occupied the Chair of Rhetoric and English Literature in the University for over twenty years and in academic circles and far beyond he brought to the University's reputation in literary scholarship the same kind of lustre which Professors William Cullen, James Syme and James Y. Simpson had earned in their own sphere for the Edinburgh Medical School. Born in Aberdeen in 1822 and educated at the Grammar School, Marischal College and Edinburgh University, he gained a high reputation in London during eighteen years there before returning to Edinburgh and taking up the English Literature Chair in 1865.

273

Masson's authorship of books, articles in leading magazines, and editorial work, was not only of a high level of scholarship, but also (which was by no means common) he had a most attractive style and was eminently readable. His leading work was perhaps *The Life of John Milton*, in several volumes, at the time regarded as a uniquely exhaustive biography. His biographies and studies of notable Edinburgh people in *Edinburgh Sketches and Memoirs* is especially fascinating. Professor Masson was particularly active in securing higher educational opportunities for women, and in 1871 he assisted in the foundation of the Edinburgh Association for the University Education of Women. In the aftermath of Edinburgh's Golden Age in literature and the arts he helped to maintain the city's high place in the world of letters. That a scholar of Professor David Masson's calibre should have graced the opening ceremony of South Morningside Primary School was a remarkable distinction. He died in 1907.

Andrew Carnegie
by D. N. Sutherland
Photograph by Norval, Dunfermline
By courtesy of the Carnegie Dunfermline Trust

ANDREW CARNEGIE

No doubt the parents present at the school opening ceremony, were suitably impressed by the magnificent achievements in the world of scholarship that were personified by Professor Masson (even if these did not move all of the rather young pupils!) However, they also had the experience of seeing and hearing one who in turn personified the greatest achievements in a quite different world — that of industry and commerce. For as such none was greater than the Fife-born Andrew Carnegie, concerning whom many phrases have been coined, about "the rags to riches story" — the boy born in a Dunfermline weaver's cottage who became the richest man in the world; the multi-millionaire who in almost legendary, fairy-tale-like manner gave away 350 million dollars.

Carnegie was born 150 years before these words are being written, in November 1835. After the emigration of his parents to the USA in 1848 he began work at the age of 13 as a bobbin boy in a Pittsburg mill for 1 dollar 20 cents a week. By studying at night-school and reading in a local library he became a telegraph-boy at 20 dollars a month and an expert in Morse code. The road to promotion and wealth which followed was by

Andrew Carnegie

His gift for the founding of the Edinburgh Central Library was originally £25,000, indicated in a letter to Edinburgh's Lord Provost Sir Thomas Clark of April 27th 1886. Only a few days later Carnegie cabled an alteration to his letter, increasing his gift to £50,000. It is the belief of the descendants of the former Lord Provost George Harrison, the immediate predecessor in office to Sir Thomas Clark, that it was Harrison's close friendship with Carnegie that had led to his most generous gift, which might have been sent direct to Harrison had he not died suddenly in 1885. Within a year of the opening of Edinburgh's Central "Free Library" on June 9th 1890, and of which Andrew Carnegie had himself laid the foundation stone, books had been borrowed by 44,774 readers. Carnegie, if he was informed of the great and speedy use made of his gift, must have been immensely gratified.

The list of Carnegie's benefactions seems limitless. In 1901, when he retired and sold out his business interests for 400 million dollars, he was the richest man in the world. He had a philosophy concerning wealth. The enterprising rich man created it in order to distribute it, but the main aim should be "to help those who help themselves". He was not without his critics concerning the means by which his wealth was acquired, especially in the British Trade Union world concerning the conduct of his USA firms and disregard for trade union rights.

way of a supervisor's job in the Pennsylvania Railroad Company, investments in oil, and iron works. By the time of the American Civil War in 1861 he was already important in the transport world and a dollar millionaire, and by 1868 — twenty years after his arrival in the USA — his fortune was enormous. Carnegie made a rule for himself that all earnings above a certain level — a not uncomfortable one! — should go each year for benevolent purposes. One of his first major benefactions was the presentation of a library to his native Dunfermline in 1881. The provision of "Free libraries" to which he had owed much of his own self-education, progress and wealth were his special interest, and it is on record that he donated 3000 of them.

Some of the key dates in Carnegie's diary published to mark the 150th anniversary of his birth indicate that he was in Scotland in 1892, at the time of South Morningside School's opening.

While not a few former pupils of the school have made their mark in Professor Masson's academic world, albeit at a humbler level, one Morningside boy, a former pupil of another local school at Churchill, emulated Andrew Carnegie's business success in India, if on a somewhat more modest scale and with a less humble beginning. This was Sir David Yule, referred to elsewhere.

HEW MORRISON

Andrew Carnegie and Hew Morrison
Opening of Central Public Library

Hew Morrison
From "Edinburgh and the Lothians at the Opening of the 20th Century" by Alexander Edington

THE third man completing a distinguished trio who participated in the South Morningside School formal opening ceremony was Hew Morrison, present as the Chairman of the St Cuthbert's and Dean School Board, one of the district education authorities which preceded the eventual setting up of the overall Edinburgh School Board.

Mr Morrison, who came to reside in Correnie Gardens in Morningside, was born in Torrisdale, Sutherland-shire, in 1849, where he attended the local Free Church school. Becoming a schoolmaster, he taught at Ardrishaig and Brechin before becoming Edinburgh's first city librarian in June 1887, three years before the Central Library in George IV Bridge actually opened. He retired in 1922 after 35 years service in this post and died in 1935. A member of many learned societies, Mr Morrison was awarded the degree of LL.D. by St Andrews University in 1904. He served as convenor of Edinburgh's Moray House Teachers' Training College Committee. Hew Morrison was an authority on Celtic literature and carried out much antiquarian studies of the Highlands.

It was Mr Morrison's enthusiasm

Children at South Morningside
Primary School c.1900

for developing educational opportunities that greatly impressed Andrew Carnegie, who saw his own generous financial provision for the opening of so very many free libraries as an important contribution towards educational development, and they became close friends. Indeed, after Carnegie had given £50,000 to the Edinburgh authorities for the opening of the city's first public library, he himself nominated his friend Mr Hew Morrison as Edinburgh's first city librarian.

10 · MORNINGSIDE WRITERS AND ARTISTS

PERHAPS as the boundaries of Morningside are now being passed and we proceed southwards to Swanston to pay tribute to the renowned Robert Louis Stevenson, it is appropriate to record some of the less outstanding writers and artists who have resided in the district. Of those who did make their mark in the literary world many have already been referred to in their various localities, such as Sir Daniel Wilson, Dr John Brown, Dr John Comrie, Dr John Hill Burton and, of course, the First World War poets Siegfried Sassoon and Wilfred Owen. That the tradition has certainly been maintained which confirms Morningside as the chosen and congenial residence of very many authors of the present day was impressively revealed a few years ago when during a community festival with a "Meet the Authors" stall local people were surprised and fascinated to discover and to converse with a large number of authors dwelling in their midst, some indeed of international "best seller" reputation in the world of fiction, and some associated with a rich and wide variety of work in other spheres.

Three authors in particular are remarkable for first providing some insight into the early days of Morningside, two of them in a rather anecdotal but nonetheless fascinating manner. One of these was Robert Cochrane in *About St Matthews, Morningside*, a booklet published in conjunction with the church's bazaar in 1908, which supplied considerable material in a selection with the heading "Memoirs of Morningside". Twelve years later, in his little classic work *Pentland Walks: Their Literary and Historic Associations*, Cochrane provided an introductory chapter rather similar in content to the St Matthews publication. It contained much interesting material and a useful bibliography enabling readers to pursue various aspects at greater depth. Little is known of Robert Cochrane, but his early writings form a valuable contribution to the history of Morningside and district.

Cover of "Robbie Doo" by Joseph Laing Waugh

Illustration by H. M. Kerr, RSA

278

Not a lot too could be found about the other early writer, Joseph Laing Waugh, again an author of a classic of its kind, *Robbie Doo*, published in 1912, and of other rather similar works such as *Thornhill and Its Worthies*, together with short stories. Waugh, who resided in 1912 at 3 Comiston Drive, was a native of Thornhill in Dumfriesshire. He was a director of an Edinburgh interior decorator's business. In *Robbie Doo*, which is based on an old man's reminiscences which include Morningside of the late 19th century, there are a number of colourfully worded descriptions of the village, with references to the old toll-house and the smiddy and a vivid recollection of the view over Edinburgh from the summit of Braid Road. There is also what Waugh in his preface calls a "touching episode" which occurred at the bridge over the Braid Burn in Braid Road near the entrance gates to the Hermitage of Braid. It is certainly a mysterious and intriguing incident that is described. The low broad stone wall overhung by a large hawthorn tree which stood beside the old toll-house and is now the site of Morningside's modern new post office is recalled. Waugh remarks in the preface to the *Robbie Doo* second edition how it had been published with some trepidation as regards likely sales and its reception by the critics; but uneasiness on both counts proved unnecessary and three thousand copies were sold within six weeks.

WILLIAM MAIR

THE third writer of some time ago

who made an important and significant contribution towards presenting a more systematic history of Morningside was William Mair, whose book *Historic Morningside: Lands, Mansions and Celebrities*, published in 1947, was widely read and indeed to a large extent pioneered the separate publication of local history studies in Edinburgh outwith those which appeared in the volumes issued by the Old Edinburgh Club. Mair's work originated as a most valuable and detailed history of Morningside Parish Church, of which he was an Elder, published in 1940, two years after the church's centenary, and which included, almost incidentally, *The Story of Old Morningside*. This material, considerably expanded, was subsequently published in Volume 24 of the Book

William Mair
by courtesy of his grand-daughter Mrs Deirdre Wedd

279

of the Old Edinburgh Club in 1942, and five years later, with some further revision, as the book entitled *Historic Morningside*. Its original cost was three shillings and sixpence. Fortunately, through the kind interest and ready assistance of Mr Mair's grand-daughter, Mrs Deirdre Wedd, these biographical notes and a portrait can be presented as a modest tribute to this Morningside historian which is long overdue.

William Mair was born in Dundee on May 11th 1868 and was educated there. After qualifying as a Member of the Pharmaceutical Society, of which he later became a Life Member, he subsequently became a dispenser and tutor in Dundee Royal Infirmary, where he also edited the hospital pharmacopoeia. Having become a Fellow of the Chemical Society, he left hospital pharmacy to join the firm of Fletcher, Fletcher & Co. of London, with whom he remained for forty years. He was latterly a leading member of their staff of representatives. This post involved him in much travel, not only in the United Kingdom, but also on the Continent and beyond. Consequently he contributed many articles, illustrated with his own photographs, to *The Chemist and Druggist*, on pharmaceutical practice in other countries, including the United States, Canada and India. In 1931 he was elected an honorary member of the American Pharmaceutical Association. In 1941 he published *An Index of New Remedies*, which he revised in 1943 and 1945. In 1948 he produced *An Index of Modern Remedies*.

For a short period William Mair was in charge of the surgical instrument department of Smith, Stanistreet & Co., Calcutta, and while there, as an expert photographer, in 1897 he himself took the first radiograph to be made in India: it was of a fractured fibula. This was only two years after Professor Röntgen's discovery of X-rays. Mair was requested by the Indian Government to purchase a unit of X-ray equipment. In collaboration with an Indian doctor Mair was co-author of a book with the title *Indigenous Drugs of India*.

Long after his special pioneering photographic work in India William Mair's skill with a camera was applied to many aspects of Edinburgh, most notably to his producing a panoramic view, by infra-red technique, of the city and beyond from the Braid Hills. This encompassed the scene within a radius of 25 miles as viewed from a point beside the flag-pole behind the original golf club-house, and 525 feet above sea-level. The enlarged photograph was placed in a large show-case-type teak frame, measuring $6\frac{1}{2}$ feet by 18 inches, on two supports and at a height which made it possible for it to be studied by children. This was designed by the City Architect, Mr E. J. MacRae, and installed in December 1936. The panorama showed a wide range of places and features of the landscape, from Dalmahoy in the west, north-west to Ben Lomond, the islands of the Firth of Forth, the towns and villages of Fife and beyond, and eastwards to Berwick Law. The places to be seen had been indicated on the photograph by Mr John Mathieson, FRSE, FRSGS, an authority on such matters. A disc indicator, also drawn by Mr Mathieson, was added giving elevations and distances. A rather similar viewing indicator had been placed in the Royal Botanical Gardens in 1920, containing a photograph by Mr Robert M. Adam, FLS, and Mr Mathieson's creations were also to be seen elsewhere in the city. Alongside the Braid Hills indicator were placed two fine teak seats, the gift of the then Councillor Mrs Morison Miller. Unfortunately Mr Mair's interesting and imaginative gift has long since been removed.

Mr William Mair, for 50 years a pharmacist, extensive world traveller, pioneer of radiography in India, noted photographer and local historian, was deservedly elected a Fellow of the Royal Society of Edinburgh and of the Royal Geographical Society. In September 1898 he married Isabella Jane Urquhart and they had a son and a daughter. The son, Dr William F. Mair, TD, MD, MRCP (Edin.), was for long a general practitioner in St Andrews until his death some years ago. Mr Mair, first writer to present a brief but valuable history of Morningside and surrounding districts, died at his home, No 32 Braid Hills Road on 1st December 1948 and was interred beside his wife, who had predeceased him, in Morningside Cemetery.

SCOTTISH LITERARY RENAISSANCE

IN recent years Morningside had also proved a congenial environment for a number of writers who have been amongst the leaders of the continuing renaissance in Scottish literature and drama, and although several of these died many years ago their work still calls for deeper appreciation and perhaps further development by others.

ALEXANDER REID

Alexander Reid
by courtesy of Mrs Genevieve Reid

THIS writer who long resided in Craiglea Drive until his death in 1982, was born in Edinburgh in 1914. After completing his education at George Heriot's School he went on to spend several years as a journalist with the Edinburgh *Evening News*, later with the *SMT Magazine* and then as editor of *The Saltire Review*. He had also worked as an accountant and bookseller; and by 1948 he was a full-time writer and broadcaster. But Reid's strong interest lay in drama and he was one of the group of Scottish playwrights much inspired by James Bridie and who, with Robert McLellan and others, sought to create or revive an authentic Scottish theatre with the Glasgow Citizens' Theatre Company which provided so many noted and talented Scots actors able most effectively to interpret such work. Alexander Reid, whilst drawing upon Scottish history and legend for much of his work, wrote: "I do not believe that Scottish history consists of Mary Queen of Scots and Bonnie Prince Charlie strutting in and out like ghosts in the Celtic twilight". He sought to present an authentic Scottish drama different from so many of today's "Scottish" playwrights whose themes are not uniquely Scottish but rather reflect aspects of life common to many British industrialised cities.

Reid's most successful play, *The Lass wi' the Muckle Mou'* was first performed by the Glasgow Citizens' Theatre Company in 1950. Set in the Borders and based upon their folklore and legends, it was greatly praised by the critics. It was performed during the Edinburgh Festival and later translated into several European languages and performed in Moscow, Croatia, the USA, Canada and Australia. The play was considered not only an important new contribution to the Scottish theatre but to British theatre as a whole. Reid's other major work was *The World's Wonder*, also first performed by the Glasgow Citizens' Company in 1953. Again with a Borders setting this play prompted the distinguished drama critic Ivor Brown to describe its author as "likely to be one of the most important of the arriving Scottish dramatists".

In his writing for the theatre Alexander Reid faced the serious problem of choice of language: whether to write in Scots, which would baffle an English audience and thus limit his appeal, or to put his work into "near English". As a dramatist Reid considered Scots-English to stem not from life but from literature. "It smelt", he said, "as did much of Stevenson's work, of printer's ink and the English Literature class". In the event the language he used in his two major plays was described as "a golden embroidery of dancing words". His work had a strong philosophical basis, especially (as in *The World's Wonder*) concerned with free will and determinism. Yet he wrote "from the heart to the heart". He published two volumes of poetry.

Alexander Reid had a profound knowledge of France where he had lived for long periods, and he wrote of that country and its life. His wife is French. In the present continuing search for the authentic nature of Scottish theatre and in the context of the need for the preservation and wider appreciation of the Scots language, Alexander Reid's work remains highly relevant and richly deserves close study.

TOM MACDONALD (FIONN MAC COLLA)

In an obituary tribute to Thomas Douglas MacDonald, who died on July 20th 1975, Hugh MacDiarmid wrote: "Having known most of the Scottish authors of the past 50 to 70 years, I have frequently said that the young writer known to me of the greatest potentiality as a creative writer was Thomas Douglas MacDonald. His death is a great loss to Scottish literature — greater, I am

Tom MacDonald

(Fionn McColla)

By courtesy of Mrs Mary MacDonald

the North-East Lowlands, Tom Mac Donald was the only Scottish novelist to achieve a synthesis of both the Highlands and the Lowlands.

Tom MacDonald — or Fionn Mac Colla as he preferred — was born in Montrose in 1906. After graduating as a teacher in Aberdeen he worked in the Gairloch area of Wester Ross and then for some time in Palestine. Returning to Scotland in 1929 he studied Gaelic at Glasgow University and became headmaster in a number of schools in the Highlands and Western Isles. Moving to Edinburgh eventually, he and his family resided for many years in Morningside Park. His novels *The Albannach* (1932) plus *And the Cock Crew* (1945) expressed his constant preoccupation with the extremes of Calvinism and his concern for its repressive influence. His own philosophy was very evident in *At the Sign of the Clenched Fist* (1967), which expanded upon the belief of Carl Gustav Jung as regards the need for a deeper understanding of human nature, taking account of Jung's conviction that "The only real danger that exists (to man) is man himself. . . . His psyche should be studied because we are the origin of all coming evil". It was Tom Mac Donald's personal preoccupation with the themes of his novels which led to his conversion to Catholicism. His deep appreciation of Gaelic culture also permeated his work, and his fervent concern was for the preservation and development of genuine Scottish culture and nationhood, which he believed could be ensured only by the establishment of an independent Scottish parliament. In recent years his work has enjoyed a renewal of interest and a new presentation.

certain, than the deaths of Compton Mackenzie, Neil Gunn, Eric Linklater and George Scott Moncrieff put together."

Praise indeed from the great Scottish poet who did not readily lavish eulogies upon many of his contemporaries; and all the more genuine and impartial perhaps since, while in fact they were very close friends, Hugh Mac Diarmid was a self-confessed Communist and Tom MacDonald an ardent convert to the Catholic Church. Mac Diarmid joined with others in considering Tom Mac Donald to be one of the architects of Scotland's national and literary resurgence. One critic wrote that while Neil Gunn was the interpreter of a section of the Highlands and Lewis Grassic Gibbons of

GEORGE CAMPBELL HAY

George Campbell Hay
Photograph: Gordon Wright

WILLIAM SHEPHERD ("SHAKES-PEARE") MORRISON, brought up in Canaan Grove in Newbattle Terrace, who became one of the most famous Speakers of the House of Commons and had his roots in South Uist, found the pomp of the daily Speaker's Procession in the House embarrassing. He revealed that frequently during the solemn ritual he would silently whistle to himself a bagpipe tune and think nostalgically of the sound of the sea in his beloved but far-off Hebrides. "Shakes" Morrison's practice often occurred to me when I met George Campbell Hay, one of Scotland's most distinguished Gaelic poets, seeing him or greeting him amid the bustle and daily commerce and deafening traffic of Morningside Road. I always felt that behind George's smile and his "on stage" appearance in the crowded streets, in fact his mind was far away, hearing the screech of the seabirds over his beloved Tarbert bay, Loch Fyne.

Few people in Morningside knew or recognised George Campbell Hay or realised just how scholarly and remarkable a man dwelt amongst them, in Maxwell Street, but he was nevertheless known to a wide readership through his published work. His considerable output of poetry in Gaelic, Scots and English has been professionally assessed elsewhere and these are but a few general notes on the man himself. George Campbell Hay was born in Elderslie in Renfrewshire on December 8th 1915. His father, John MacDougall Hay, was born in Tarbert, Loch Fyne, son of a shipping agent, and had a brilliant career at Glasgow University where he gained many prizes and distinctions. After graduating in Arts he taught for some time in Stornoway and Ullapool. In 1905 he returned to Glasgow University to study for the ministry of the Church of Scotland. Again his University performance was distinguished. He was appointed to a parish at Elderslie. There he wrote many articles for magazines and other publications but he became best known for his novel *Gillespie*, first published in 1914 and reprinted in 1962 and 1979 when it became a minor best seller and indeed created a more or less sensational reaction, based as it was on the squalid side of life of a Scottish village, recognisable to many as Tarbert. It was said that as a consequence of his novel he was asked to resign from his ministry in the church but refused to do so. He died of tuberculosis in the year 1919.

George Campbell Hay inherited his father's literary and poetic talents. Though the latter did not speak Gaelic, young George's mother did. George and his mother spent many summers in Tarbert and there he learned Gaelic from his aunts. He came to reside with his mother in Edinburgh in 1925 and attended John Watson's School. In 1929 he became a Foundationer at Fettes College, and he was provided with an entirely free education. At Fettes he was completely uninterested in mathematics and science but showed an unmistakable taste for literature: indeed much of the college magazine was written by himself under a variety of pen-names. In 1934 George won a Major Scholarship in Classics to Corpus Christi College, Oxford. After leaving Oxford, he attended Edinburgh's Moray House Teachers Training College and subsequently taught Latin and Greek at the Royal High School for a short period. At the outbreak of the Second World War in 1939 George, who was an ardent Scottish Nationalist, refused to be conscripted on the grounds of conscientious objection, as did fellow-Nationalist Douglas Young. After his appeal for exemption was rejected, George Campbell Hay "went on the run" in the hills of Argyll, but was caught and for a short period was interned in Saughton Prison in Edinburgh. Eventually he joined the Royal Ordnance Corps.

In 1942 Hay was serving in North Africa, Tunisia and Algeria, where he learned Arabic and Italian to add to his already considerable linguistic ability. While in Italy he acted as an interpreter. Later, serving in Macedonia, he learned modern Greek and through his liking for the Greek people was found fraternising with them more than the authorities approved and was wrongly suspected of being a Communist agitator. Consequently he was the victim of an attack with knives and guns. This experience seriously affected him mentally and he was invalided out of the army. For his war service George Campbell Hay was awarded the 1939-1945 Star, Africa Star with Clasp, the Italy Star and the Defence Medal.

Hay was sent initially to a hospital at Lochgilphead, then later to the Royal Edinburgh Hospital. Despite expert psychiatric treatment, there were fears for George's future health. However, he did recover considerably and worked for a short time in the Antiquarian Division of the Department of Printed Books in the National Library of Scotland, where he also lodged many of his notebooks. He returned to his poetry and had four collections published between 1947 and 1982. He received the Gaelic Writers Award from *An Comunn Gaidhealach* in 1982. As already noted, Hay was not a native Gaelic speaker and had mastered the language not only from his aunts in Tarbert but from his having spent so many happy days there going out on Loch Fyne with the Tarbert fishermen whom he came to love greatly. These days are commemorated in one of the poems with which these notes conclude, while the other reveals his preoccupation with landscapes. He made many allusions to European poetry and translated much of it into English and Gaelic.

George Campbell Hay's nostalgic escape from the noise and

distractions of Morningside Road was no negative, uncreative thing. Often he would say to me: "There's something stirring way down in the depths o' my mind . . . I think there's a poem beginning to form in all this". And, as for so many great artists, no attempt at escapism could ever free him from the state of " . . . no respite from the terrible tyranny of the Muse". George Campbell Hay died alone in his house in Maxwell Street on March 25th 1984. His going was a great loss to his friends and to Scotland.

Of Kintyre he wrote: "I have loved your sea and moorland, the bareness of your hills under the blue of the sky, the shimmer of sun on their fair-sided flanks, old garden of sweetest and kindliest nature. Sweet is the voice of the wind on your mountains, crying on their high shoulders; lovely your white belt about you, the sea closing in on the shore".

From *The Old Fisherman*:

Greet the bights that gave me shelter,
they will hide me no more with the
horn of their forelands.
I peer in a haze, my back is stooping;
my dancing days for fishing are over.

The shoot that was straight in the
wood withers,
the bracken shrinks red in the rain and
shrivels,
the eyes that would gaze in the sun
waver;
my dancing days for fishing are over.

The old boat must seek the shingle,
her wasting side hollow the gravel,
the hand that shakes must leave the
tiller;
my dancing days for fishing are over.

The sea was good night and morning,
the winds were friends, the calm was
kindly —
the snow seeks the burn, the brown
fronds scatter;
my dancing days for fishing are over.

Finally, to the youth of Scotland: "Youth of my country, is it to be the tranquillity of the plains, then, the peace and slumber of the low valleys, sheltered from the rough blast? Let your step be on the summit, and your breast exposed to the sky. For you the tearing wind of the pinnacles, lest destruction come on us like a land-slide."

DR STUART MACGREGOR

WHILE George Campbell Hay and Alexander Reid, different as they were in in background and in the object of their work, found so much of their material and inspiration in Scotland's ancient traditions and

The Old Fisherman

were fascinated by language and imagery, the fourth of the Morningside group of writers very much part of a more modern literary scene lived in a very different personal world which was the stuff of his novels and poetry. It was the distinctive world of University life in Edinburgh, undergraduate and graduate, in its leisure hours, of relationships, sometimes critical and intense, of serious philosophical discussions and reflections in well-known student pubs, notably "Sandy Bell's" in Forrest Road, where more serious moods could switch naturally and rapidly to the gaiety of tavern folk song and happy camaraderie.

Dr Stuart Mac Gregor, who was educated at George Heriot's School, graduated in Medicine in 1959, and from 1964 was on the staff of the University's Department of Social Medicine — now Community Medicine — at the Usher Institute, for some time specialising in the epidemiology of alcoholism. In January 1973, while engaged in a two-year contract in the Department of Social and Preventative Medicine in Kingston, Jamaica, he was tragically killed in a car accident. His career in, and contribution to, medical research alone would have been praiseworthy and satisfying enough for most men, and indeed the sense of loss among his medical colleagues was profound, such were Mac Gregor's achievements and his dynamic personality; but like A. J. Cronin and James Bridie and other medicals-turned-authors, with whom he has been compared, he was by his own confession a compulsive writer, "no respite from the terrible tyranny of the Muse". At his tragic death when he was only 37 his literary career had barely begun. His wife, a native of North Uist, to whom he attributed so much inspiration and encouragement, showed me a considerable collection of manuscripts which, one hopes, may still find a publisher.

Stuart Mac Gregor's first novel, *The Myrtle and the Ivy*, written while in the army and published in 1967 is a lively, rather down-to-earth tale of Edinburgh student life, to some degree autobiographical. Following the publication of a selection of his poetry, along with that of Sorley MacLean, George Campbell Hay and William Neil, in *Four Points of a Saltire* (1970), Mac Gregor's second novel, *The Sinner*, was published posthumously in 1975. It is a study in conflict between the intellectual approach and intuition, between

Dr Stuart MacGregor

Photograph: Gordon Wright

287

genuine folk music and commercialised art, with Edinburgh again as the setting. Combining his excursions into fiction and poetry with a lively love of folk music, Stuart Mac Gregor, together with Jean Redpath and Hamish Henderson of the University's School of Scottish Studies, was involved in the founding in 1958 of the Edinburgh University Folksong Society and Mac Gregor was elected the first president. A song of his own about Sandy Bell's bar reached the USA and Canada. His early death was certainly a serious and tragic loss to Scottish literature and the arts.

MORNINGSIDE ARTISTS

MANY painters, in oils and water-colours, have resided in Morningside, especially in the latter half of the 19th century. Some of these have already been referred to in some detail, such as Miss Hannah C. Preston Magoun and Sam Bough. Of the others only sparse information could be traced, except for one who was found to have been resident, presumably as a tenant, at Greenbank farm-house in about 1880. This was Robert Alexander, RSA. The farmhouse seems to have existed from somewhat earlier times, possibly before 1800, and Greenbank farm's lands were at that time quite extensive and productive. The house seems to have stood at the west end of what is now Greenbank Avenue and its pleasant setting would be attractive to an artist. Robert Alexander enjoyed a high reputation for his animal subjects. James Caw in his *Scottish Painting: Past and Present: 1620-1908* comments that

Robert Alexander

by J. R. Abercromby

By courtesy of the National Galleries of Scotland, Edinburgh

animal painting in Scotland had failed to become a real and vital art until Alexander began his work. This may seem a surprising and controversial statement since long before Alexander, who was born at Kilwinning, had forsaken house-painting for pictorial art, another notable artist who had associations with Greenhill and Morningside, and who is buried in the cemetery here, Gourlay Steell, RSA, had been appointed Queen Victoria's Animal Painter for Scotland and also a painter to the Highland and Agricultural Society. He was appointed Curator of the National Gallery of Scotland in 1882. His elder brother was the celebrated Sir John Steell who resided in Greenhill Gardens. Caw, while praising Steell's accurate, objective, and conventional representational painting of

288

Gourlay Steell

Braid Iron Church (1884)

animals, felt that it lacked the more imaginative qualities of Alexander's work. By 1884 Alexander had moved from Greenbank to Canaan Grove, now No 82 Newbattle Terrace.

Although a certain amount of biographical detail and portraits of Robert Alexander and Gourlay Steell exist, unfortunately such could not be traced for the many other artists who resided or worked in Morningside. These include Frederick Dove Ogilvie, whose home was in Belhaven Terrace and who produced a fine water-colour with a sense of life and warmness of the original Braid "iron church" which stood at the corner of what is now Braid Road and Cluny Gardens. He also painted two water-colours of the original *Volunteers Rest* at the corner of Canaan Lane, the early *Volunteer Arms* or *Canny Man*, which are among Morningside's first hostelry's interesting collection of treasures from its past. In Woodburn Terrace resided James Kinnear, whose characteristic initials appear in several Edinburgh scenes and possibly in at least one of Morningside. Another artist was Diaz, who painted the area at the entrance to the Hermitage of Braid, looking north. Robert McGregor, RSA, who resided for some time at Bloomsberry Cottage in Canaan was buried in Morningside Cemetery. He illustrated many books for Thomas Nelson and Son.

11 · COMISTON

THE Comiston district can lay claim to very early historic associations, in the possible origins of its name and in the Caiystane or Cammo Stone, described by most authorities as simply "A stone marking the grave of some commander killed in an ancient battle". But in the relatively more recent history of Edinburgh, Comiston holds a special place as the source of the city's first piped water supply brought from the district in 1681 to the great tank at Castlehill, via what is now the Braidburn Valley Park, the entrance area of the Hermitage of Braid Park, Canaan Lane, Whitehouse Loan, Marchmont, the Meadows, Grassmarket and finally, steeply uphill by Castle Terrace to Castlehill. This was an impressive feat of civil engineering for three centuries ago. Although clearly a number of people predominantly participated in various capacities in the introduction of this important new health-giving facility to the street wells of the old town, details and portraits of only a few are extant.

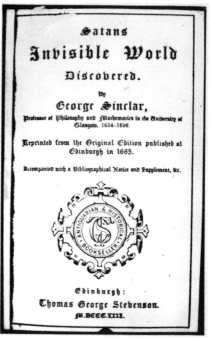

Title Page of Notable Book by George Sinclare

GEORGE SINCLARE

A "Schoolmaster at Leith", he was an expert in "Hydrostaticks" and dedicated a book on this subject in 1683 to Sir James Fleming, Lord Provost of Edinburgh. There is some confusion in the records concerning Sinclare's Christian name. In some accounts he is named John and in others George. In 1685 he published a rather remarkable book: *Satan's Invisible World Discovered*, which dealt, not with "hydrostaticks", but with witchcraft and demoniacal possession, in various countries, and including the bizarre activities of the notorious Major Weir in Edinburgh. In the preface of this book, the author has signed himself as George Sinclare. Prior to his appointment as a Leith schoolmaster in mathematics, Sinclare was for some time Professor of Philosophy and Mathematics at Glasgow University.

In the early 1670s, when Edinburgh Town Council were searching for a source of spring water which could be brought to the city, Sinclare's services, in the application of mathematics to the civil engineering involved, were enlisted. In May 1674 as a result of his studies he established that the ground at Comiston, the source of many springs to be drawn upon, was 200 feet higher than Castlehill where the collecting tank would be situated and therefore "the sweet waters of Comiston" could be piped to Castlehill by gravity. It has been suggested that the cannon-ball to be seen embedded in the west wall of Cannonball House, facing the Castle esplanade, was not lodged there by a defence gun during an attack on the Castle but was in fact placed there, possibly by Sinclare, to mark the point at which the nearby Castlehill tank was 200 feet lower than Comiston.

Sinclare was commissioned by the city authorities to collaborate with Peter Bruschi, a Dutch engineer, in the process of piping the water from Comiston. In the Town Treasurer's Accounts for 1673-74 appears the entry: "Item to Mr Jon Sinclare, schoolmaster at Leith, by gratuitie for his attendance and advyce in the matter of the waterworks, £66.13.4d".

Sinclare died in 1693. Information about his parentage, birthplace and early life is uncertain, but it is known that his brother was minister of the church at Ormiston in 1646, and was treated favourably by Cromwell during his invasion of Scotland and given certain jurisdiction in Lothian, Merse and Teviotdale. George Sinclare experimented in various branches of science, especially physics and hydrostatics, and reputedly produced a type of diving-bell used in 1655 in Tobermory Bay in an attempt to salvage the treasures of a Spanish galleon believed to have been sunk there.

BAILIE JAMES COLSTON

Bailie James Colston
Etching by A. J. Featherstone
From "The Edinburgh and District Water Supply: A Historical Sketch" by James Colston

WHILE a number of brief historical accounts of the Comiston water supply and of the many subsequent substantial additions to that original source, from Swanston springs to the most recent addition of the Megget supply, have been written by officials of the water supply authorities, anyone wishing to go back to the earliest details of Edinburgh's sources will normally be referred to "Colston", the name synonymous with the historical presentation on the subject. The full title is: *The Edinburgh and District Water Supply. A Historical Sketch*, written by James Colston in 1890 and it is certainly the most thorough treatment of the subject. It contains considerable introductory material on the importance of an adequate water supply "essential for countering two great threats": in fire-fighting, in the old town, a frequent requirement, and "for health reasons, especially in eradicating plagues of various kinds". Colston philosophises on the vital role of water in life generally and references to Greece, Rome and Pompeii find a place in his writings.

James Colston served on Edinburgh Town Council for nearly 30 years and was involved both in the proposal and the implementation of many new developments in the city. He was the younger son of Alexander Colston, printer, and was educated at the High School where he won many distinctions. To his regret his father virtually compelled him to become a printer but he certainly broke out of the confines this might have imposed by entering the Town Council in 1866, thereupon beginning a long and notable career in public service. Bailie Colston had strong personal views on many public issues of his day. He favoured the building of the Usher Hall at the end of the West Meadows near Brougham Street, rather than at Lothian Road, since the former being city property would have been a free site. He never believed that the Usher Hall could be an economic asset. His book on the Edinburgh and District Water Supply was written at the request of the city's Water Trustees and he was deeply involved in the lively debates concerning further sources such as St Mary's Loch. He was responsible for the development of West Princes Street Gardens, was Honorary Secretary of the Royal Infirmary when it was a voluntary hospital, and was responsible for raising large sums for contributions and other enterprises as also for various causes such as relief after a disaster in Lancashire, a fire in Chicago, and a famine in China. He served on the University Court. Very much a book-man, Bailie Colston had a uniquely large library on the history of Edinburgh. By his own authorship he added to these through: *A History of the Incorporation of the Trades of Edinburgh*; *A History of the Scott Monument*; *A History of Trinity College, Church and Hospital*; and a work on the relationship between Edinburgh and the Port of Leith.

SIR JAMES FORREST

THE Lady Colmestone, with whom Edinburgh Town Council negotiated for access to the many springs within her land — "presenting her annually with the best silk gown that money could buy" — was the widow of Walter Porterfield, an advocate. She herself was of the ancient Edinburgh family of Cant, who had once owned the Grange of St Giles, and she had inherited Comiston from her father, John Cant. In 1715 Comiston passed from the Porterfields to a family which was to be associated with the estate for nearly a century and a half. The first of these, James Forrest, was a Leith merchant who soon after-wards acquired the nearby lands of Dreghorn and whose son, James, in turn also purchased the adjacent lands of Oxgangs. Yet another James, the subject of this note, succeeded to Comiston and built Comiston House, as the present-day house was originally known, in 1815

Lord Provost Sir James Forrest

— described as "a neat country villa, typical of its time" but nevertheless with interesting architectural features. It is now known as the Pentland Hills Hotel.

James Forrest qualified as an advocate in 1803, and after entering the Town Council became a pioneer and supporter of many public causes. He was Lord Provost from 1837 until 1843 and was created a Baronet in 1838. Soon after his election as Lord Provost he summoned a public meeting to petition Parliament to introduce voting by ballot in local government elections, as a safeguard against voters being pressurised. While still Lord Provost, the Disruption occurred in 1843, as a result of which very many people "came out" or seceded from the Established Church of Scotland to form the Free Church of Scotland. Sir James Forrest was among the great many prominent public figures and Town Councillors who joined the Free Church. The campaign for the abolition of road tolls in Scotland also received Forrest's strong support; although this was not to occur until 1883 he did succeed in having the toll transferred southwards from near Wrychtishouses to the former "Briggs O' Braid" at the foot of Morningside Road, on account of the increasing number of people moving out to the south to reside there and resenting the payment of toll fees on leaving and re-entering the area.

As the masonic Grand Master of Scotland Sir James Forrest laid the foundation stone of the Scott Monument on August 15th 1840. Forrest Road was named in his honour. Perhaps the most dramatic and certainly the most embarrassing occasion in Sir James's career, although not without its amusing side, was the *contretemps* which occurred in 1842 during Queen Victoria's first visit to Edinburgh. The Royal party arrived at Granton Harbour slightly earlier than scheduled, to find no official reception party of the Lord Provost and his bailies. The Queen did not wait, but set out for Dalkeith Palace for a few days before entering the city. Sir James Forrest and the city dignitaries immediately left for Dalkeith. Their embarrassment and profound apologies before the Royal visitor can easily be conjectured, but soon all was forgiven. The incident did give rise, however, to not a few rhymes and songs. One of these was a parody on *Hey, Johnnie Cope*.

Hey, Jamie Forrest, are ye waukin
yet?
Or are your Bailies snorin' yet?
If ye are waukin, I would wit
Ye'd hae a merry, merry mornin'!
The Queen she's come to Granton
Pier,
Nae Provost and nae Bailies here:
They're in their beds I muckle fear
Sae early in the mornin'!

Sir James Forrest died in 1860, aged
81, and was buried in Greyfriars
Churchyard a short distance from the
entrance to the Covenanters' Prison.
Forrest Road, a continuation southwards of George IV Bridge, was
named in this Lord Provost's
honour, as has been noted.

THE SIX-FOOT-HIGH
CLUB

"HARD by at the back of Comiston",
wrote Stevenson in *Edinburgh:
Picturesque Notes*, "a belated carter
beheld a lady in white, with the most
beautiful clear shoes upon her feet,
who looked upon him in a very
ghastly manner and then vanished".
The ghost of Comiston House!
"And just in front", Stevenson
continues," is the *Hunters' Tryst*,
once a roadside inn, and not so long
ago haunted by the Devil in
person..." After describing in rather
whimsical fashion the panic caused
to the inn's *clientèle* by the super-
natural visitations, characterised by
loud bangs and moans and groans,
R.L.S. relates that certain clergy were
brought out specially from the city to
exorcise the hostelry of its
unwelcome guest. In much later years
the explanation was advanced by a
writer in the magazine of Dreghorn

College, an establishment at one
time not far from the inn, that the
uncanny noises heard therein had a
possible quite natural explanation.
Pipes carrying spring water from
Bonaly to Edinburgh apparently
passed underneath, or very close to,
the inn, and in dry weather, which
caused sparse or irregular water
supplies, air locks formed in the
pipes, and this, together with wind
blowing through them, gave rise to
the uncanny sounds.

Be Stevenson's account as it may,
in the 1820s, fifty years before he had
come to know *Hunters' Tryst*, they
were not ghostly figures who
frequented the inn and its vicinity but
a company of men of real flesh and
blood and, most notably, all were at
least six foot tall. Hunters' Tryst was
for long the *rendezvous* of the Six-
Foot-High-Club. While membership
was officially restricted to "six-
footers", many exceptions were
made, especially when those
admitted of lesser stature brought
fame and honour to the club. Such
examples, from the literary world,
were Sir Walter Scott, James Hogg
(the Ettrick Shepherd), who was the
club's poet laureate, John Lockhart,
Scott's son-in-law and biographer,
Christopher North, and others.
Another honorary member of the
club was none other than Stevenson's
Monsieur Saint-Yves, hero of the
famous novel, who having escaped
from Edinburgh Castle and after his
concealment at Swanston Cottage,
set off uphill by what is now
Swanston Road and into present-day
Oxgangs Road, where he saw a light
in what he discovered to be Hunters'
Tryst inn, and where members of the
Six-Foot-High Club were in the
midst of an all-night sitting, imbibing

Dress Uniform of the Six Foot High Club

From "Old Edinburgh Characters and Costumes"
by J. G. Howie c.1830-1840
By courtesy of Edinburgh City Archives

and singing merrily. The disguised French officer was cordially given temporary club membership.

Sir Walter Scott was in fact appointed the umpire of the club, which office perhaps provides a clue to its predominant activities, *viz.* the practice of Scotland's national games, athletic contests and gymnastics. The club's gymnasium was at East Thistle Street and later at Malta Terrace. The summer athletic contests were held in a field beside the inn. A report of a contest appearing in the *Edinburgh Courant* for May 10th 1828 details such events as "putting an iron bullet of 21 pounds"; throwing a sledge hammer; hop, step and leap; and races of one mile and three miles. The performances recorded would match, if not better, present-day Olympic standards! The club's "dress uniform", of which illustrations remain, was of "the finest dark green cloth coat, double-breasted with special buttons and a velvet collar. The vest was of white Kerseymere and the trousers were white. On special occasions a tile hat was worn." The club was appointed Guard of Honour to the Hereditary Lord High Constable in 1828.

295

12 · SWANSTON

HILAIRE BELLOC, in his classic *The Path to Rome*, must have tantalised many readers when, having completed his lengthy pilgrimage on foot through Europe, by way of villages, mountain-paths and many obstacles, when at last within sight of his objective, Rome, he stopped short and for reasons explained to his lector, simply gazes down upon the Eternal City, without entering and beginning to deal with its history. Belloc makes no apology. Rome has been written about so often and in such detail. What can he add? The same temptation arises as the top of Swanston Road is at last reached and one gazes down upon Swanston itself. So much has already been written about the village and its setting; and biographies of Robert Louis Stevenson himself abound, and even now new versions are frequently appearing.

Something of the history of the place is given in an earlier volume. These pages are concerned with people. So many associated with Swanston come to mind. It must be remembered that the village had its own existence and way of life long before the Stevenson family first came here in the summer of 1867, and remained for nearly fourteen years, during which it so influenced and impressed young Louis that for this reason it has become immortal. For a very long time Swanston farm was an important one, with sheep, cattle and a variety of crops.

The Stevenson Family

Alison Cunningham ("Cummy") is on young R. L. S.'s left
By courtesy of the City of Edinburgh Museums

THE STEVENSON FAMILY

THE weakness in health which plagued Robert Louis Stevenson from his earliest days and during which he was so devotedly nursed by "Cummy" never left him and was to result in his premature death. It is probable that it was the hoped-for benefits of the country air and wholesome farm produce of Swanston which influenced his parents to obtain a lease of Swanston Cottage, where they lived for 14 summers from 1867 until 1880. It can only be presumed that in fact the pleasant setting of the cottage and the other advantages did benefit young Louis physically. Certainly his years at Swanston profoundly inspired him spiritually and intellectually and occasioned some of his finest descriptive writing, notably in *Edinburgh: Picturesque Notes* and *Memories and Portraits*.

There are no records of how Stevenson's father, busily engaged in his lighthouse designing, travelled from Swanston to and from his office in the city, nor how Mrs Stevenson, perhaps in Cummy's company, went on shopping visits to the town. From the foot of Morningside Road, horse-drawn buses had become available during the years the family was at Swanston. Stevenson himself, then attending the University, briefly to study, first of all engineering, and then law, seemed to walk in frequently by the banks of the Braid Burn and on through Morningside, and, it would seem, used often to return to Swanston again on foot. Thus he was for long a familiar figure to the villagers of Morningside, with his velvet jacket and stooped shoulders. The Stevenson family were well known at the little post-office at Fairmilehead.

JOHN TODD

John Todd the Swanston Shepherd with his third sheepdog "Trusty"

TWO people contributed greatly to Stevenson's literary inspiration and in the formative period of his development. The first, in point of time, and from his own admission of most decisive influence, was Cummy, who did so during his most susceptible years of childhood and boyhood. And she was with him, of course, at Swanston during his years there. The other person of importance was John Todd, the Swanston shepherd. After Stevenson's first arrival at the cottage his initial encounter with Todd was not at all cordial. He would scale the wall surrounding the large garden and make his way into the village and up towards Caerketton. The tone of Todd's voice when Louis first heard it was not too pleasant! He was rather angrily commanding Louis' dog Coolin to "C'war oot amang the sheep!" Before long, however, the strong, tireless shepherd and the pale, slight, teenage student became the best of friends: so much so that Todd, before setting off up the hillside, would come past Swanston Cottage wall, give his distinctive whistle and Stevenson would appear in a flash and, together, with their dogs, they would make for Halkerside, Caerketton or Allermuir.

Stevenson developed the utmost affection and admiration for his friend, who fascinated him with his anecdotes and recollections of his days as a drover taking his flocks through the Borders and across into England, sleeping rough on the hillside, falling victim to robbers, once being wrongly jailed but managing to escape. This was excellent material for a future novelist and master of adventure stories. It all fired Stevenson's imagination, as did Todd's manner of speaking. "He spoke in the richest dialect of Scots I've ever heard". And none of Todd's wealth of stimulating material was lost, for as he himself once remarked to his young friend, Adam Ritchie, a Swanston ploughman: "He's an awfu'laddie for speirin questions aboot a'thing, an' whenever ye turn yer back, awa' he gangs an' writes it a'doon!" Much of what Stevenson "wrote doon" and later sculpted into shape at the desk in his bedroom in Swanston Cottage was preciously to enrich the world's literary heritage. John Todd was born at Friarton on the lands of Spittal between Habbie's

Howe at Nine Mile Burn and the Carlops. He was a shepherd there for a few years before moving to Swanston. Various descendants of Todd remain and with them a living archive of the Swanston shepherd and his family. His wife Ann Somerville and one of their children are to be seen in an early photograph of the villagers.

AN OLD SCOTS GARDENER

Robert Young – "An Old Scots Gardener"

Photograph by James Patrick

APART from John Todd, the Swanston shepherd, who had far-reaching influence on Stevenson both personally and as regards his future writing, and to whom the author paid fitting tribute in *Memories and*

Portraits, another Swanston "character" whom Stevenson chose to immortalise, and seemed to be intent on doing so, again in *Memories and Portraits*, was Robert Young, to whom he devoted a whole, if brief, chapter under the title "An Old Scots Gardener". Indeed Stevenson wrote: "Now as I could not bear to let such a man pass away with no sketch preserved of his old-fashioned virtues, I hope the reader will take this as an excuse for the present paper and judge as kindly as he can the infirmities of my description." Stevenson continued that it was impossible to think of Swanston Cottage with its garden "in the lap of the hills" without also seeing Young's wrinkled face, stooped back and "his spare figure and old straw hat". The garden and gardener seemed "part and parcel of each other".

Stevenson related that considering where Robert Young had worked earlier in life, his domain at Swanston Cottage was very small and humble compared with the gardens of the "grand houses, castles and parks" where he had been in charge and where under-gardeners had trembled at his looks. After occupying such an elevated position it seemed it was a condescension on his part to dress humbler garden plots. Yet Robert Young maintained his sense of importance and he decided just what the Swanston Cottage garden would produce. "He would fill the most favoured and fertile section of the garden with certain vegetables that none of us could eat, in supreme contempt for our opinions".

Although the old gardener preferred almost exclusively traditional flowers such as sunflowers, dahlias, wallflowers and roses, he made one exception — wild foxgloves. These were allowed to thrive without interference. "And yet", wrote Stevenson, "the very truth was that he scorned flowers altogether. They were but garnishings, childish toys, trifling ornaments for ladies' shelves. It was towards his cauliflowers and peas and cabbages that his heart grew warm. His preference for the more useful growths was such that cabbages were found invading the flower pots and an outpost of savoys was once discovered in the centre of the lawn".

A man of deep religious beliefs, Robert Young applied his form of theology to his gardening. If he was complimented upon a plant's fine appearance, he would humbly touch his hat and express grateful appreciation. If, however, the garden showed failures, he would quote Scripture: "Paul may plant and Apollos may water". Blame was attributed to Providence on the grounds of insufficient rain or an untimely frost! Eventually, Stevenson solemnly relates, the earth which the old gardener had so often dug was dug out by another for his burial. And near to the grave of the faithful old servant the flowers seemed to grow better, and for "The Last Post" a bird from the hillside flew twittering over his open grave.

THE REAL AND THE ROMANTIC

WHEN Stevenson was spending his summers at Swanston Cottage and came to know the villagers and their cottage homes he was eventually to

A Swanston farm worker and his wife
at their cottage door

describe it all as a "romantic" scene in the chapter "To the Pentland Hills" in his *Edinburgh: Picturesque Notes* and this may well have been so when he was writing in 1878. Half a century earlier, William Somerville in his *Autobiography of a Working Man*, and other social commentators of the time, presented a life-style for farm workers and their families such as those at Swanston in a rather less than romantic view. And the first Swanston cottages having been built long before Somerville's day, existing presumably in 1745 when the Jacobite soldiers passed through the village as records relate, then living conditions would have been rather primitive, at variance with the picturesque "chocolate box" scene one might be tempted to envisage. The cottages indeed have been described as having one main room 13 feet by 12 feet, a privy and an adjoining midden. Some had an extra closet-room with space for the parents' bed. For long they had no flooring, only the bare earth. Add to these features the long working-day of the farm labourers, the prevalence

A group of Swanston villagers
John Todd's wife, holding their young son, is seen seated second from the left in the second row
By courtesy of the late Mrs J. Slater

of large families to be brought up in such limited accommodation and with such inadequate facilities, and certainly in the earliest period there could have been little romanticism in the scene.

Stevenson, however, writing more than a century after Swanston's beginnings, was to relate of the cottages: "Some of them (a strange thing in Scotland) are models of internal neatness; the beds adorned with patchwork, the shelves arrayed with willow-pattern plates, the floors or tables bright with scrubbing or pipe-clay, and the very kettle polished like silver. . . . Housework becomes an art; and at evening, when the cottage interior shines and twinkles in the glow of the fire, the housewife folds her hands and contemplates her finished picture; the snow and the wind may do their worst, she has made herself a pleasant corner in the world". With all its natural features, in the lap of the hillside, its domestic scene, its "characters" and its hard-working people, this was the Swanston which Stevenson so vividly described, dearly loved and could never forget.

Lord Charles Guthrie
From "Lord Guthrie: A Memoir"
by Sheriff Robert L. Orr

LORD GUTHRIE

IN 1881 the Stevensons gave up the lease of Swanston Cottage. In the previous year Louis had married Mrs Fanny Osbourne, and after spending a few years in Europe from 1884-1887 they spent much of the time at Bournemouth, where Stevenson completed a good deal of his writing. After a few visits to Edinburgh, notably for the funeral of his father on May 13th 1887, with his wife, mother and stepson

he set out for New York and then finally Vailima, where he died in 1894. After the Stevensons' departure from Swanston, the cottage which was the property of the Edinburgh Water Trust, became the residence for some time of the City Water Engineer, and then in 1908 it was leased to a man who had been a close friend and deep admirer of Stevenson. This was Lord Guthrie, Senator of the College of Justice.

Charles Guthrie, born at No 2 Lauriston Lane on April 4th 1849, was the 6th son and 10th child of the Reverend Thomas Guthrie, DD, Minister of the Free St John's Church near the Castle. His mother, Ann Burns, was the daughter of one of the ministers of Brechin Cathedral. The father, Dr Guthrie as he was familiarly known in Edinburgh, became famous as a preacher, philanthropist and for his practical concern for the children of poor families. He was the pioneer of the various "Ragged Schools", and campaigned for reforms to help the poor. Charles Guthrie was educated at the Southern Academy in George Square and later in Park Place, then at the High School. At the University, as a fellow law student he became a close friend of Stevenson, who graduated in the subject and became an Advocate, although he never practised. Both were members of the famous and exclusive Speculative Society. Guthrie became an Advocate in 1875 and eventually a Judge in 1907.

Such had been Guthrie's admiration for Stevenson that not only had he been most eager to acquire a lease of Swanston Cottage, but when he moved in he began converting the house into a Stevenson museum, collecting prints, portraits and letters, even acquiring a large wooden wardrobe made by Deacon Brodie — Stevenson's prototype for *Dr Jekyll and Mr Hyde* — which was eventually transferred from Swanston Cottage to the Stevenson collection in the Lady Stair's House museum. Lord Guthrie built a small bungalow for his son and his family beside Swanston Cottage.

Lord Guthrie was also a very close friend of Cummy's and in 1908, about 15 years after she had left her brother's cottage at Swanston to live in Balcarres Street, the Duchess of Sutherland, who was visiting Edinburgh, was invited by Lord Guthrie to dine at Swanston Cottage. He also arranged for Cummy to be brought out to the cottage, where she met the

Alison Cunningham ("Cummy")
with Lord Charles Guthrie at the Quarry Garden,
Swanston Cottage
Photograph by James Patrick
By courtesy of the City of Edinburgh Museum

Duchess and they were photographed together outside the door. Cummy was not at all pleased at the breach of protocol. Later, when she was shown the photograph, she remarked pointedly: "Look at that! — fancy me being photographed with a Duchess and me sitting while she's standing". Lord Guthrie was also photographed with Cummy at the Quarry Garden, a favourite haunt of Stevenson's. The Judge wrote a small booklet, *Cummy: The Nurse of Robert Louis Stevenson. A Tribute to the Memory of Alison Cunningham*. It was published as a memorial shortly after her death in July 1913. Lord Guthrie was amongst the small group of close relatives and friends who attended her funeral at Morningside Cemetery

Alison Cunningham ("Cummy")

with the Countess of Sutherland at Swanston Cottage: 1908

were at Swanston. I would like fine to go up the burnside a bit and sit by the pool and be young again — or no, be what I am still, only there instead of here, for just a little. Some day climb as high as Halkerside for me (I am never likely to do it for myself again) and sprinkle some of the well water on the turf. I am afraid it is a Pagan rite but quite harmless, and ye can be sain it wi' a bit prayer. Tell the peewees that I mind their forebears well. My heart is sometimes heavy and sometimes glad to mind it all...".

Of the very many people associated with South Edinburgh none have loved the district or Edinburgh itself more dearly than Stevenson. His memories of Swanston and the places he passed as he walked to and fro are perhaps expressed most vividly in these lines:

> I gang nae mair where aince I gaed,
> By Buckstone, Fairmilehead or
>   Braid,
> But far frae Kirk and Tron,
> Oh, still ayont the muckle sea,
> Still are ye dear and dear to me,
> Auld Reekie, still and on.

Of the Pentland Hills and Rullion Green:

> Blows the wind today and the sun
>   and the rain are flying
> Blows the wind on the moors today
>   and now.
> Where about the graves of the
>   martyrs the whaups are crying,
> My heart remembers how.
> Grey recumbent tombs of the dead
>   in desert places.
> Standing stones on the vacant
>   wine-red moor.
> Hills of sheep, and the howes of the
>   silent vanished races.
>   and winds, austere and pure.

on July 21st 1913. He also wrote a most interesting book on Stevenson published in 1924, full of anecdotes and personal reminiscences not found in most of the official biographies, and it contains a number of photographs. He died on April 28th 1920.

No matter the happiness he enjoyed in his new life in Vailima, Stevenson could never forget Swanston and his favourite parts of the hillside above the village. From Bournemouth, before leaving Britain for America, he wrote to Cummy: "As I write, there is a blackbird singing in our garden trees as if it

303

Be it granted to me to behold you
again in dying.
Hills of home! and to hear again
the call;
Hear about the graves of the
martyrs the peewees crying,
And hear no more at all.

Finally, the places which haunted
him:

The tropics vanish, and meseems
that I
From Halkerside, from topmost
Allermuir
Or steep Caerketton, dreaming,
gaze again.
Far set in fields and woods, the
town I see.
Springs gallant from the shadows
of her smoke,
Cragged, spired and turreted, her
virgin fort.
Beflagged. About on seaward
drooping hills,
New folds of city glitter. Last, the
Forth.
Wheels, ample water set with
sacred isles,
And populous Fife smokes with a
score of towns.

Robert Louis Stevenson

The voice of generations dead
Summons me, sitting distant, to
arise,
My numerous footsteps to retrace,
And, all mutation over, stretch me
down
In that denoted city of the dead.

SELECTED BIBLIOGRAPHY

VOLUME 3

SIR THOMAS HOPE OF RANKEILLOR *(p. 1)*
Memorial Thomas Hope of Rankeilor 27th May, 1761, manuscript; Whalley, Fred, *(Letter to Charles J. Smith concerning 6 Hope Park Square, containing a map, plan and illustration, 12th August, 1983,)* typescript

WILLIAM BURNESS *(p. 4)*
Burns, Robert, *The Life and Works; ed. by Robert Chambers, Vol. 1*, Edinburgh, W. & R. Chambers, 1856; Lindsay, Maurice, *The Burns Encyclopedia*, London, Hutchinson, 1959

WILLIAM MILLER OF MILLERFIELD *(p. 5)*
M(iller), W(illiam) F(rancis), *A Catalogue of engravings by William Miller*, H.R.S.A., *1818 to 1871*, London, Simmons & Botten, 1886

WILLIAM DICK *(p. 9)*
Bradley, Orlando Charnock, *History of the Edinburgh Veterinary College*, Edinburgh, Oliver & Boyd, 1923; Phillips, J. E., "Veterinary medicine — 19 years old but with a 160 year history", *University of Edinburgh Bulletin, Vol. 19, No. 5*, Edinburgh, University of Edinburgh, June 1983

LADY JANET HEPBURN *(p. 14)*
Seton, George, *The Convent of Saint Catherine of Sienna, near Edinburgh*, Edinburgh, privately printed, 1871

LORD HENRY COCKBURN *(p. 19)*
Cockburn, *Lord* Henry Thomas, *Memorials of His Time*, Edinburgh, Foulis, 1909

REVEREND MOSES JOEL *(p. 20)*
Phillips, Abel, *A History of the origins of the first Jewish community in Scotland – Edinburgh 1816*, Edinburgh, John Donald, 1979

JAMES GOODFELLOW *(p. 22)*
Goodfellow, James, *The Print of His Shoe*, Edinburgh, Oliphant, Anderson & Ferrier, 1906; Newington United Presbyterian Church, (a) *Quarterly records*, Edinburgh, N.U.P.C., various dates; (b) *Annual report of the missionary, educational and benevolent institutions . . . for the year ending 31st October, 1869*, Edinburgh, James Taylor, 1870 (c) *Jubilee Memorial, 1848-1898*, Edinburgh, R. W. Hunter, 1898

ELIZA WIGHAM *(p. 25)*
Mein, Elizabeth M., *Miss Eliza Wigham: notes from various sources*, N.d., typescript

ROBERT MIDDLEMAS *(p. 27)*
Middlemass, R. & Son Ltd., *Jubilee Year, (1869-1919)*, Edinburgh, Middlemas, 1919.

DR BENJAMIN BELL *(p. 29)*
Bell, Benjamin, *The Life, character and writings of Benjamin Bell*, Edinburgh, Edmonston & Douglas, 1868

DR ROBERT KNOX *(p. 31)*
Stephen, Kathy, *Scottish Men of Medicine: Robert Knox* M.D., F.R.S.E. *(1791-1862)*, Edinburgh, History of Medicine and Science Unit, 1981; Knox, Frederick John, *Preparations illustrative of the whale . . . now exhibiting in the Pavilion, North College Street*, Edinburgh, Neill & Co., 1838; *The Blue Whale – balaenoptera musculus* (Royal Scottish Museum NH 1864.49), typescript; Edwards, Owen Dudley, *Burke and Hare*, Edinburgh, Polygon Books, 1980

EUGENE CHANTRELLE *(p. 35)*
Smith, A. Duncan, ed. *Trial of Eugène Marie Chantrelle*, Glasgow, William Hodge, 1906

WILLIAM BLACKWOOD *(p. 39)*
Oliphant, Margaret Oliphant Wilson *Annals of a publishing house: William Blackwood and his sons, their magazine and friends*, 3 vols., Edinburgh, Blackwood, 1897

ROBERT KIRKWOOD *(p. 41)*
Robertson, R. A., "Medals, medallions and a' that", *Edinburgh Yearbook*, Edinburgh, Scott Hamilton, 1957; Moir, D. G. rev., *The Early Maps of Scotland to 1850. . .*, Vol. I; 3rd ed., Edinburgh Royal Scottish Geographical Society, 1973

DAVID OCTAVIUS HILL *(p. 45)*
Scottish Arts Council, *A Centenary*

exhibition of the work of David Octavius Hill, 1802-1870 and Robert Adamson, 1821-1848; selection and catalogue by Katherine Michaelson, Edinburgh, Scottish Arts Council, 1970; Hill, David Octavius and Adamson, Robert, *An Early Victorian Album: the Hill/Adamson Collection; ed. . . . by Colin Ford*, London, Cape, 1974; Gill, Arthur T., "Hill and Adamson", *The Photographic Journal, Vol. 117, No. 1* London, The Royal Photographic Society, Jan/Feb, 1977; Anderson, William S., "D.O. Hill's disruption painting" *The Monthly Record of the Free Church of Scotland*, Edinburgh, April 1984

JOHN ALEXANDER LONGMORE *(p. 49)*

John A. Longmore Trust, *Sederunt Book, 1875*, manuscript; *Longmore Hospital*, n.d., typescript; *History of Longmore Hospital*, Edinburgh, Gordon Wilson, n.d.; The Royal Edinburgh Hospital for Incurables, Royal Charter of incorporation Edinburgh, Mackenzie & Black, 1903

JAMES C. H. BALMAIN *(p. 52)*

"Pioneer photographer: death of Mr James C. H. Balmain", *Edinburgh Evening News, June 24, 1937*; "Putting back the clock: photographs from the Balmain Collection", Edinburgh, *Scotland's S.M.T. Magazine*, December, 1952

JOHN GEORGE BARTHOLOMEW *(p. 54)*

Allan, Douglas A., "John George Bartholomew", *The Scottish Geographical Magazine*, Vol. 76, No. 2, Perth, The Royal Scottish Geographical Society, 1960 Gardiner, Leslie, *Bartholomew 150 years*, Edinburgh, John Bartholomew & Son Ltd, 1976

SIR THOMAS DICK LAUDER *(p. 60)*

Lauder, Sir Thomas Dick, *Scottish Rivers*, Glasgow, Morison, 1890

DAVID BRYCE *(p. 64)*

Fiddes, Valerie & Rowan, Alistair, *David Bryce, 1803-1876*, Edinburgh, University of Edinburgh, 1976

ROBERT M. BALLANTYNE *(p. 66)*

Catford, E. F., "A Hundred years since the first of R.M.B.", *Edinburgh Evening News, September 10, 1955*; Quayle, Eric, *Ballantyne the Brave: a Victorian writer*

and his family, London, Rupert Hart-Davis, 1967

DR HORATIUS BONAR *(p. 70)*

Maxwell, Thomas, *St Catherine's in Grange*, 1866-1966, Edinburgh, Bishop & Sons, 1966.

JAMES BUCHANAN *(p. 72)*

Duncan, Flockhart, & Co., *The History of Duncan, Flockhart & Co., Commemorating the Centenaries of Ether and Chloroform*, Edinburgh, Duncan, Flockhart & Co. 1947; Chambers, Robert, *Lives of illustrious and distinguished Scotsmen, Vol III, Pt. 1*, Glasgow, Blackie & Son, 1833

BISHOP JAMES GILLIS *(p. 77)*

Gordon, J. F. S., *Journal and appendix to Scotichronicon and Monasticon*, Glasgow, John Tweed, 1867; *History of St Margaret's Convent, Edinburgh, the first religious house founded in Scotland . . .*, Edinburgh, John Chisholm, 1886

SISTER AGNES TRAIL *(p. 80)*

Trail, Agnes Xavier, *Conversion of Miss Trail, a Scotch Presbyterian: written by herself*, London, Catholic Truth Society, 1897

DR SOPHIA JEX-BLAKE *(p. 82)*

Todd, Margaret, *The Life of Sophia Jex-Blake*, London, Macmillan, 1918

SIR GEORGE WARRENDER *(p. 83)*

The Times, "Obituary of Sir George Warrender", *The Times, June 14, 1901*; Weir, Robert B., *A History of the Scottish American Investment Company Limited, 1875-1973*, Edinburgh, Scottish American Investment Company, 1973

MARGARET WARRENDER *(p. 86)*

Bruntisfield, Lord, (*Letter to Charles J. Smith concerning Margaret Warrender, 3rd September, 1983*), manuscript; Foster, Stewart, (*Letter to Charles J. Smith concerning Margaret Warrender, 9th December, 1983*), typescript; Stewart Douglas F., (*Letter to Charles J. Smith concerning Margaret and Alice Warrender, January 8, 1985*), typescript

SIR JOHN USHER *(p. 91)*

A History of the Usher Family in Scotland, Edinburgh, privately printed, 1956; Maclean, Una, *The Usher Institute and the evolution of community medicine in Edinburgh*, Edinburgh, Department of Community Medicine, University of Edinburgh, 1975

ALEXANDER MCKELLAR *(p. 93)*
Kay, John, *A Series of Original Portraits,* 2 vols., Edinburgh, Hugh Paton, 1837

MARY BARCLAY *(p. 96)*
Churches (Scotland) Act Commission Order No. *1180: Miss Mary Barclay Trust,* Edinburgh, H.M.S.O., 1909; Ewing, William, ed. *Annals of the Free Church of Scotland, 1843-1900,* 2 v., Edinburgh, T. & T. Clark; *The Monthly Record of the Free Church of Scotland,* Edinburgh,Turnbull & Spears, July 1924; *Barclay Church Supplement,* Edinburgh, the Church, 1965

SIR WILLIAM FORBES OF PITSLIGO *(p. 99)*
Ryan, Terence M., *(Letter to Charles J. Smith concerning Sir John Stuart Forbes, 8th Bt. of Pitsligo, March 11, 1984)* manuscript

DAVID COUSIN *(p. 101)*
Edinburgh Corporation, *Report on the duties and emoluments of the principal officials in the service of the Corporation of the City of Edinburgh,* Edinburgh, Turnbull & Spears, 1870; "The Late Mr David Cousin", *Edinburgh Courant, 4 September 1878;* Smith, John, *Greenhill Gardens, Bruntsfield Links: With Notes on Some of its Early Residenters,* manuscript, 1930; Smith, John, *Notes on the Lands of Greenhill, Bruntsfield Links and their Owners,* manuscript, n.d.; Macrae, E. J., *Historical review of the City Architect's Department of the City of Edinburgh, 11th February, 1937,* typescript; Anderson, William S. "Two historic windows", *The Monthly Record of the Free Church of Scotland,* Edinburgh, Free Church of Scotland, July/August, 1984

PROFESSOR ARCHIBALD H. CHARTERIS *(p. 106)*
Gordon, Arthur, *The Life of Archibald Hamilton Charteris.* London, Hodder & Stoughton, 1912

ELIZA W. KIRK *(p. 109)*
Kirk, E. W., *Book of Tried Favourites,* Selkirk, Lewis, 1900; Kirk, Logan, *(Letter to Charles J. Smith, concerning Mrs Kirk, March 28, 1985,)* manuscript

ANDREW USHER *(p. 110)*
A history of the Usher Family in Scotland, Edinburgh, privately printed, 1956

HIPPOLYTE JEAN BLANC *(p. 112)*
Building News and Engineering Journal, Vol. LVIII, no. 1846, London, 1890; Royal Scottish Academy, *Ninetieth Annual report of the Royal Scottish Academy of painting, sculpture and architecture,* Edinburgh, T. & A. Constable, 1917

GEORGE SETON *(p. 115)*
"The Late Mr George Seton, advocate", *Scots Law Times,* Vol. 16, pt. 26, Edinburgh, C. E. Green, November, 1908

JOHN NAPIER *(p. 118)*
Napier, Mark, *Memoirs of John Napier of Merchiston,* Edinburgh, Blackwood, 1834; *Napier College, Edinburgh* (brochure), n.d.

CHARLES CHALMERS *(p. 120)*
Merchiston Castle School Register, 1833-1929, Edinburgh, Pillans & Wilson; Keir, David, *The House of Collins: the story of a Scottish family of publishers from 1789 to the present day,* London, Collins, 1952

SIR JAMES GOWANS *(p. 123)*
McAra, Duncan, *Sir James Gowans, romantic rationalist,* Edinburgh, Paul Harris, 1975

THEODORE NAPIER *(p. 124)*
Napier, Theodore, *The Royal House of Stuart. . . ,* Edinburgh, Balmanno, 1898; Eddington, Alexander, *Edinburgh and the Lothians at the opening of the twentieth century,* Brighton, Pike, 1904

GEORGE WATSON *(p. 125)*
Waugh, Hector, L., ed., *George Watson's College: history and record, 1724-1970,* Edinburgh R. & R. Clark, Ltd., 1970

DR THOMAS CHALMERS *(p. 128)*
Brown, Thomas, *Annals of the Disruption,* Edinburgh, Macniven & Wallace, 1895; Stephen, Kathy, *Scottish Men of Letters: Thomas Chalmers (1780-1847), F.R.S.E.,* Edinburgh, History of Medicine and Science Unit, 1981

JANE WELSH CARLYLE *(p. 130)*
National Library of Scotland, *Thomas Carlyle, 1795-1881,* Edinburgh, N.L.S., 1981

SUSAN FERRIER *(p. 132)*
Ferrier, Susan Edmonstone, *Memoir and Correspondence of Susan Ferrier 1782-1854,* ed. John A. Doyle, London, John Murray, 1889; Parker, William Mathie, *Susan Ferrier and John Galt,* London, Longmans Green, 1965; National

Library of Scotland, *Susan Ferrier, 1782-1854*, Edinburgh, 1982

LT. COLONEL DAVID DAVIDSON *(p. 134)*

Davidson, David, *Memories of a long life*, Edinburgh, David Douglas, 1890

SIR DANIEL WILSON *(p. 137)*

Hannah, Hugh, "Sir Daniel Wilson: the man and his work", *Book of the Old Edinburgh Club*, Vol. XVII, Edinburgh, T. & A. Constable, 1930

PROFESSOR GEORGE WILSON *(p. 140)*

Wilson, Jessie Aitken, *Memoir of George Wilson*, Edinburgh, Edmonston & Douglas, 1860

SIR DAVID YULE *(p. 142)*

Mudie, Sir Francis, *Andrew Yule & Co: notes for a projected book on "The Scots in India"*, manuscript, n.d.; *George Yule & Company, 1865-1920, Yule Catto & Company Limited, 1920-1963*, Edinburgh, T. & A. Constable, 1963; *The Squire of Hanstead: an historical record of the Yule Family and the Hanstead Estate*, St Albans, Ambassador College, 1973

ARCHBISHOP COSMO GORDON LANG *(p. 145)*

Lockhart, J. G., *Cosmo Gordon Lang*, London, Hodder & Stoughton, 1949

HANNAH C. PRESTON MACGOUN *(p. 147)*

Caw, James L., *Scottish Painting Past and Present, 1620-1908*, Edinburgh, Jack, 1908

MARY CARLYLE *(p. 149)*

The Homes and haunts of Thomas Carlyle, London, *Westminster Gazette*, 1893; Davidson, Mabel, "A Lady who deserves to be remembered", *The Sewannee Review*, Vol. 31, July, 1923; Carlyle, Alexander, *Jottings on Alexander Carlyle's Life and Work*, 1931, typescript; Carlyle, Mary (Mary Carlyle Aitken), *Scottish song: a selection of the choicest lyrics of Scotland*, London, Macmillan & Co., 1874

WILLIAM "SHAKESPEARE" MORRISON *(p. 152)*

Mackenzie, Alexander, "Mr Speaker", *The Watsonian*, Edinburgh, Watsonian, May, 1952; Allan, James C., *(Letter to Charles J. Smith concerning William*

Shepherd Morrison, 24th., May, 1983), manuscript; Campbell, Neil, "William Shepherd Morrison (1893-1961)", *University of Edinburgh Journal (Vol. XXXI, no. 1)*, Edinburgh University of Edinburgh Graduates' Association, June 1983; Moir, D. G. ed., *The Early maps of Scotland to 1850, Vol. 2*, Edinburgh, Royal Scottish Geographical Society, 1983

ALEXANDER FALCONAR *(p. 156)*

Falconar, Alexander, *Letter book, 1787-1796*, manuscript; Princep, Charles C., *Record of services of the H.E.I.C.'s civil servants in the Madras Presidency*, 1885; Davidson, Alexander, *Family letter book, (c 1742-91)*, manuscript; Davidson, Elizabeth, *Journal (1788-89)*, manuscript

JAMES GRANT *(p. 159)*

H. A. R, "James Grant, prolific historian and antiquarian", *Edinburgh Evening News, June 17, 1933*; Foster, Stewart, *The Catholic Church in Ingatestone, from the Reformation to the present day*, Great Wakering, Mayhew-McCrimmon, 1982; Foster, Stewart, *James Grant: a forgotten novelist*, n.d., typescript; Foster, Stewart, *(Letter to Charles J. Smith concerning James Grant, November 23, 1983)*, typescript; Boag, William G. F., *(Letters to Charles J. Smith concerning James Grant, December 1, 1983)*, typescript

DAVID DEUCHAR *(p. 160)*

Deuchar, Alexander, *(Letter to Charles J. Smith concerning David Deuchar containing notes and a family tree, November 3, 1984)*, manuscript

ANNIE S. SWAN *(p. 163)*

Swan, Annie S., *My life: an autobiography*, London, Nicholson & Watson, 1934; *The Letters*: ed. by Mildred Robertson Nicoll, London, Hodder & Stoughton, 1945

VOLUME 4

EBENEZER GAIRDNER *(p. 167)*

Dunlop, Alison Hay, *Anent Old Edinburgh . . .*, Edinburgh, R. & H. Somerville, 1890

THOMAS GLADSTONES *(p. 168)*
Checkland, S. G., *The Gladstones: a family Biography, 1764-1851*, London, Cambridge University Press, 1971

ROBERT FERGUSSON *(p. 169)*
Law, Alexander, *Robert Fergusson and the Edinburgh of His Time*, Edinburgh, City Libraries, 1974

DR ANDREW DUNCAN *(p. 169)*
Rosner, Lisa M., *Scottish Men of Medicine, Andrew Duncan, M.D., F.R.S.E. (1744-1828)*, Edinburgh, History of Medicine and Science Unit, 1981

DR WILLIAM McKINNON *(p. 171)*
"Obituary of William MacKinnon", *Aberdeen Journal*, January 31, 1849; *St Nicholas Churchyard, Aberdeen, memorial inscriptions*, n.d.; *Aberdeen Lunatic Asylum Minutes, 1837*, GRHB 2/1/4, manuscript; Aberdeen Lunatic Asylum, *Medical report to the managers, for the year ending April 30, 1839*, Aberdeen, D. Chalmers & Co., 1839; *(Extracts from the old parochial registers of Aberdeen, Parish of St Nicholas, referring to William McKinnon)*, various dates, manuscript; *Fasti Academiae Mariscallanae Aberdonensis: selections from the records of the Marischal College and University, 1593-1860; ed. by Peter John Anderson, Vols. 1 and 2*, Aberdeen, The New Spalding Club, 1889 and 1898; *A Directory of the city of Aberdeen, and its vicinity, 1837-38*, Aberdeen, D. Chalmers & Co., 1837; MacKinnon, Lachlan, *Recollections of an old lawyer*, Aberdeen, D. Wyllie & Son, 1935; MacKinnon, G.D.G., *(Letter to Charles J. Smith concerning William McKinnon with a family tree, 12 July, 1984)*, manuscript; MacKinnon, G.D.G., *(Letter to Charles J. Smith concerning Dr William McKinnon, July 23, 1984)*, typescript; Henderson, *Sir* David Kennedy, *The Evolution of psychiatry in Scotland*, Edinburgh, E. & S. Livingstone, 1964

DR PHILIPPE PINEL *(p. 173)*
Journal of Mental Science, "Unveiling of a bust of Pinel at the Royal Hospital, Morningside, Edinburgh, by the French Ambassador," *Journal of Mental Science*, London, Adland & Son, October 1930

SIR HENRY JARDINE *(p. 174)*
Royal Edinburgh Hospital, *Sir Henry Jardine of Harwood (1766-1851)*, typescript

GEORGE MEIKLE KEMP *(p. 176)*
Bonnar, Thomas, *Biographical Sketch of George Meikle Kemp*, Edinburgh, Blackwood, 1892; Holmes, Nicholas M. McQ., and Stubbs, Lyn M., *The Scott Monument: a history and architectural guide*, Edinburgh, City of Edinburgh Museums and Art Galleries, 1979; Barclay, John B., "The Scott Monument: a world-famous memorial," Edinburgh, *S.M.T. Magazine*, Vol. 9, *No. 3*, September 1932; Eadie, Douglas, "Man and monument", Glasgow, *Scottish Field, Vol. 118, no. 824*, 1971

SAM BOUGH *(p. 177)*
Gilpin, Sydney, *Sam Bough, R.S.A., Some account of his life and works*, London, George Bell & Sons, 1905; Mackay, John, "Sam Bough", *Scotland's Magazine, Vol. 60, No. 11* Edinburgh, November 1964; *STV Festival Art Exhibitions 1978: All about Eve . . . also centenary tribute Sam Bough (1822-1878)*, Scottish landscapes, 1978

DAVID RAMSAY HAY *(p. 179)*
"Death of Mr D. R. Hay", *The Scotsman*, December 12, 1866; "The Late Mr D. R. Hay", *The Scotsman*, December 13, 1866; Gow, Ian, "The First intellectual house-painter (David Hay)", *The World of Interiors*, London, Pharos Publications, May 1984

HENRY KINGSLEY *(p. 180)*
Huxley, Elspeth *(compiler)*, *The Kingsleys: a biographical anthology*, London, Allen & Unwin, 1973; Mellick, J.S.D., *The Passing guest: a life of Henry Kingsley*, St Lucia, New York, University of Queensland Press, 1983

WILLIAM RITCHIE *(p. 182)*
The Glorious privilege: the History of "The Scotsman", Edinburgh, Nelson, 1967

ELIZA FLETCHER *(p. 183)*
Fletcher, Eliza, *Autobiography, with letters and other family memorials*, Edinburgh, Edmonston & Douglas, 1875

SIR FRANK MEARS *(p. 186)*
Sir Frank Mears: obituary, *Royal Institute of British Architect's Journal, 3rd series,*

Vol. 60, No. 5, London, R.I.B.A., March 1953

JOHN BEUGO *(p. 189)*
Guy, John C., "Edinburgh engravers", *Book of the Old Edinburgh Club*, Vol. IX, Edinburgh, Constable, 1916

PROFESSOR JAMES SYME *(p. 190)*
Paterson, Robert, *Memorials of the life of James Syme*, Edinburgh, Edmonston & Douglas, 1874; Shepherd, John A., *Simpson and Syme of Edinburgh*, Edinburgh, E. & S. Livingstone, 1969

LORD LISTER *(p. 192)*
Fisher, Richard Bernard, *Joseph Lister, 1827-1912*, London, Macdonald & Jane's, 1977

DR JOHN BROWN *(p. 193)*
Masson, David, *Edinburgh Sketches and Memories*, London, A. & C. Black, 1892; Brown, Dr John, *Letters of Dr John Brown; with Letters, from Ruskin, Thackeray and others*, London, A. & C. Black, 1907

ALEXANDER JAMES ADIE *(p. 195)*
Royal Society of Edinburgh, *Proceedings*, Vol. IV, No. 50, Edinburgh, the Society, 1859-60; Bryden, D. J., *Scottish scientific instrument makers, 1600-1900*, Edinburgh Royal Scottish Museum, 1972; Devlin-Thorpe, Sheila, ed., *Scotland's Cultural Heritage, Vol. 1: One Hundred Medical and Scientific Fellows of the Royal Society of Edinburgh elected from 1783 to 1832*, Edinburgh, University of Edinburgh, 1981; Swann, Alexander H., *(Letter to Charles J. Smith concerning the Adie family at Canaan Cottage, containing a family tree, February 1983)*, manuscript; Swann, Alexander H., *(Letter to Mr Copeland, Chief Administrative Officer, Astley Ainslie Hospital, with notes concerning the Adie family, at Canaan Cottage, 11th November 1983)*, typescript; Campbell, Neil, *(Letter to Charles J. Smith concerning Alexander Adie, 3rd March, 1984)*, typescript

CHARLES MACLAREN *(p. 196)*
The Glorious privilege: the history of "The Scotsman", Edinburgh, Nelson, 1967

DAVID AINSLIE *(p. 198)*
Family tree of David Ainslie, typescript, n.d.; Morden, Robert Lyle Price, *Border Bairns: an Ainslie family history*, Woodstock, 1978

SYDNEY DOBELL *(p. 199)*
Dobell, Sydney, *The Poetical Works, Vol. 1*, London, Smith, Elder & Co., 1875

JAMES WILSON *(p. 200)*
Hamilton, James, *Memoirs of the life of James Wilson of Woodville*, London, James Nisbet & Co., 1859; Stuart, Marie W., "Chronicles of a garden", *Edinburgh Evening News*, September 2, 1950

THOMAS CAMPBELL *(p. 201)*
Beattie, William, ed., *Life and letters of Thomas Campbell, Vol. 1*, London, Edward Moxon, 1849

SIR JAMES RUSSELL *(p. 202)*
"Sir James Russell, LL.D.", *Edinburgh Citizen and Portobello Advertiser*, 1882-83

CANON JOHN GRAY *(p. 202)*
Sewell, Brocard, *In the Dorian Mode: a life of John Gray, 1866-1934*, Padstow, Tabb House, 1983; MacGregor, Geddes, "Poet and Priest: In the Dorian Mode: a Life of John Gray, 1866-1934," *Book World*, No. 25, Vol. 3, No. 1, Winscombe, Polybooks, February 1984

ANDRE RAFFALOVITCH *(p. 202)*
Healy, Philip, "Raffalovich and his circle, part 2 — The Making of an Edinburgh Salon", *Book World, No. 26, Vol. 3, No. 2*, Winscombe Book Advertiser, March/April 1984

SIR GEORGE WASHINGTON BROWNE *(p. 205)*
"Sir George Washington Browne: a notable Scots architect", *Journal of the Royal Institute of British Architects, Vol. 47, No. 7*, London, R.I.B.A., July 1939; Crossland, James Brian, *Victorian Edinburgh*, Letchworth, Wayfair Publishers, 1966

SIR THOMAS BOUCH *(p. 207)*
The Illustrated London News, November 13, 1880; *Tay Bridge Souvenir*, Edinburgh, The Scotsman Publications Ltd., 1966; Prebble, John, *The High girders*, London, Secker & Warburg, 1966

MENIE TROTTER *(p. 211)*
Trotter, Menie, *(Letters to Peggy Black, Edgehead, March 1 and July 11, 1835)*, manuscript; Gray, W. Forbes, "Blackford House, its literary memories," *The Scotsman*, March 5, 1938

SIR GEORGE HARRISON *(p. 213)*
(Miscellaneous papers concerning Sir George Harrison,) various dates;

Garibaldi, Guiseppe, "Letter to George Harrison, Lord Provost of Edinburgh, 11 July, 1860" *The Scotsman*, 24 December, 1885

LOUIS AGASSIZ *(p. 214)*
Agassiz, Elizabeth Cary, ed., *Louis Agassiz, his life and correspondence, Vol. I*, Boston, Houghton, Mifflin & Company, 1885; McAdam, A. D., *A Guide to Blackford Hill and its geology*, Edinburgh, Edinburgh Geological Society, 1984

PROFESSOR CHARLES PIAZZI SMITH *(p. 217)*
Brück, Hermann A., *The Story of astronomy in Edinburgh from its beginnings until 1975*, Edinburgh University Press, 1983

CHARLES GORDON OF CLUNY *(p. 220)*
Bulloch, John Malcolm, *The Gordons of Cluny, from the early years of the eighteenth century to the present time*, privately printed, 1911; *Proceedings of the Society of Antiquaries of Scotland*, Edinburgh, National Museum of Antiquities of Scotland, 1981

SIR JOHN SKELTON *(p. 222)*
Skelton, Sir John, *The Table Talk of Shirley*, Edinburgh, Blackwood, 1896

PROFESSOR CHARLES G. BARKLA *(p. 274)*
Whittaker, *Professor* E. T., "Death of pioneer in physics: Professor C. G. Barkla", Edinburgh, *The Scotsman*, October 24, 1944; "Dr C. G. Barkla, F.R.S. : obituary", *The Times*, October 25, 1944; Horton, Frank, "Professor C. G. Barkla, F.R.S. ", reprinted from *Nature, Vol. 154*, London, Macmillan & Co., 1944; Horton, Frank, "Obituary notice: Charles Glover Barkla, F.R.S. ", *Proceedings of the Physical Society*, Vol LVII, part 3, London, May 1945; Allen H. S., "Charles Glover Barkla, 1877-1944", reprinted from *Obituary notices of Fellows of the Royal Society, Vol 5*, London, the Society, 1947

JOHN McDOUGAL *(p. 226)*
The Scotsman, May 19, 1938; The Scotsman, "Edinburgh benefactor: death of Mr John McDougal," *The Scotsman*, August 2, 1949; Oddie, John, "The Man who gave the city a park", *Evening News*, February 1, 1984

THE CLERKS OF PENICUIK *(p. 229)*
Clerk, *Sir* John, *Memoirs of the life of Sir John Clerk of Penicuik, Baronet Baron of the Exchequer extracted by himself from his own journals, 1676-1755*. Edinburgh, the University Press, 1892.

JAMES S. BENNET *(p. 231)*
Fraser, Margaret E., *(Letter to Charles J. Smith concerning James S. Bennet containing an article on her father and four photographs, February 5, 1984)*, manuscript; Bennet, James S., *The Buckstane: Its History and Romance*, Edinburgh, Edinburgh Corporation Libraries & Museums Committee, 1964

THOMAS TROTTER *(p. 234)*
Good, George, *Liberton in ancient and modern times*, Edinburgh, Andrew Elliott, 1893; *Book of the Old Edinburgh Club, Vol. XI*, Edinburgh, T. & A. Constable, 1922; Trotter *Major* Alexander, *(Letter to Charles J. Smith containing notes on Thomas Trotter, 7th Bt. of Mortonhall and Charterhall, July 1985)* typescript

DR RATCLIFFE BARNETT *(p. 236)*
Greenbank United Free Church Magazines, December 1913-February, 1914, with references to T. Ratcliffe Barnett Edinburgh, the Church, 1913-1914; Greenbank Church, Edinburgh, *Congregational leaflet*, November, 1938, Edinburgh, The Church, 1938; "City minister and author (Rev. T. Ratcliffe Barnett)", *Evening News*, October 29, 1975; Macnicol, Malcolm, ed., *Princess Margaret Rose Orthopaedic Hospital*, 1982

WILLIAM A. COCHRANE *(p. 236)*
(The article on Dr Ratcliffe Barnett and Mr William Cochrane is a joint one); Ross, James A., *The Edinburgh School of Surgery after Lister*, Edinburgh, Churchill Livingston, 1978

THE GAUGER'S FRIEND *(p. 239)*
Stevenson, Robert Louis, *Edinburgh: Picturesque Notes*, various editions; as Picturesque Old Edinburgh, Charles Skilton, 1984

ALISON CUNNINGHAM *(p. 243)*
Guthrie, *Lord* Charles John Guthrie, *"Cummy", the nurse of Robert Louis Stevenson: a tribute to the memory of Alison Cunningham*, Edinburgh, Otto Schulze & Company, 1913; Cunning-

ham, Alison, *Cummy's Diary, preface
and notes by R. T. Skinner*, London,
Chatto & Windus, 1926

ALEXANDER LOW BRUCE *(p. 244)*
Keir, David, *The Younger Centuries: the
story of William Younger and Co. Ltd.,
1749-1949*, Edinburgh, McLagan &
Cumming, 1951

DR JOHN D. COMRIE *(p. 246)*
Comrie, John D., *History of Scottish
Medicine to 1860*, London, Baillière,
Tindall & Cox, 1927; "John Dixon
Comrie, M.A., B.Sc., M.D.", *The British
Medical Journal*, London, B.M.A., 14
October, 1939; "J. D. Comrie:
obituary", *The British Medical Journal*,
21 October, 1939; "John Dixon Comrie:
obituary", London, *The Lancet*, 14
October, 1939; "John Dixon Comrie:
obituary", London, *The Lancet*, 21
October, 1939; S. W. J., "Obituary,
John Dixon Comrie, M.A., B.Sc., M.D.,
F.R.C.M.Ed.", *Edinburgh Medical Journal*,
Vol. 46, Edinburgh, Oliver & Boyd,
1946.

GEORG LICHTENSTEIN *(p. 248)*
The Late Mr Georg Lichtenstein, *The
Scotsman*, February 14, 1893
SIR EDWARD APPLETON *(p. 248)*
Ratcliffe, J. A., "Sir Edward Victor Apple-
ton: obituary", Edinburgh, *Yearbook
of the Royal Society of Edinburgh*, 1964-
65; Ratcliffe, J. A., "Edward Victor
Appleton, 1892-1965, elected F.R.S.,
1927", *Biographical Memoirs of Fellows
of the Royal Society*, London, the Royal
Society, 1966
DR DOUGLAS STRACHAN *(p. 249)*
New College, *The Windows in the Library
Hall*, Edinburgh, C. C. & A. T. Gardner,
n.d.; *Stained glass windows of Douglas
Strachan*, n.p., n.d.; Wilson, William,
"Obituary notice of Douglas Strachan",
*Journal of the British Society of Master
Glass-Painters*, Vol. XI, No. 1, London,
The Society, 1961; Wilson, William,
"Douglas Strachan', *Life and Work*,
Edinburgh, Church of Scotland, March,
1951; Webster, Gordon, "Douglas
Strachan", *Journal of the British Society
of Master Glass – Painters, Vol. XIV, No.
1*, London, The Society, 1964
TOMMY ARMOUR *(p. 252)*
"The Scots Autocrat at the Corner Table",

The Scotsman, October 19, 1963;
"Tommy Armour awarded Frank
Moran Trophy", *The Scotsman*, August
30, 1963; "Frank Moran Golf Trophy,
Tommy Armour the 'Silver Scot' who
became a legend", *The Scotsman*,
August 30, 1963; Mair, Norman,
"Tommy Armour, golfing adventurer,"
The Scotsman, December 27, 1977

DR ROBERT MOREHEAD *(p. 254)*
Morehead, Charles, ed., *Memorials of the
life and writings of the Rev. Robert Morehead, D.D.*, Edinburgh, Edmonston &
Douglas, 1875

DR JOSEPH BELL *(p. 255)*
Eddington, Alexander, *Edinburgh and the
Lothians at the opening of the twentieth
century . . .* Brighton, Pike, 1904;
Robarts, F. H., "The Origins of
paediatric surgery in Edinburgh",
*Journal of the Royal College of Surgeons
of Edinburgh, Vol. 14*, Edinburgh, The
College, November, 1969; Lellenberg,
Jan L., ed., "Has anything escaped
me?" *Baker Street Miscellanea, No. 32*,
Chicago, Sciolist Press, Winter, 1982;
Liebow, Ely, *Dr Joe Bell: model for
Sherlock Holmes*, Bowling Green
University Popular Press, 1984;
Edwards, Owen Dudley, *The Quest for
Sherlock Holmes: a biographical study of
Sir Arthur Conan Doyle*, Edinburgh,
Mainstream Publishing, 1983
DR THOMAS CLOUSTON *(p. 258)*
*Quasi Cursores: portraits of the high
officers and professors of the University
of Edinburgh . . .* Edinburgh, the
University Press, 1884; "Obituary: Sir
Thomas Clouston, LL.D., M.D., F.R.C.P.E.",
Edinburgh Medical Journal, Vol. XIV,
No. 5, Edinburgh, Oliver & Boyd, 1915;
Henderson, Sir David Kennedy, *The
Evolution of psychiatry in Scotland*,
Edinburgh, E. & S. Livingstone, 1964
DR JOHN HILL BURTON *(p. 260)*
Burton, John Hill, *The Book – hunter etc.,
new ed.*, Edinburgh, William Blackwood
& Sons, 1882; Skelton, Sir John, *Essays
in history and biography. . .* , Edinburgh,
William Blackwood & Sons, 1883;
Masson, David, *Edinburgh sketches and
memories*, London, A. & C. Black, 1892
THE MONRO DYNASTY *(p. 263)*
Comrie, John D., *History of Scottish
Medicine to 1860*, London, Ballière,

312

Tindall & Cox, 1927; *The Buckle*, May, 1968, Edinburgh, Lindsay & Co., 1968; Wright-St Clair, Rex E., *Doctors Monro: a Medical Saga*, London, The Wellcome Historical Medical Library, 1964

JAMES BELL *(p. 263)*
Eddington, Alexander, *Edinburgh and the Lothians at the opening of the twentieth century*, Brighton, Pike, 1904

SIEGFRIED SASSOON *(p. 265)*
"Siegfried Sassoon at Craiglockhart", *Edinburgh Evening News*, 20 July 1957; Kerr, Douglas, "Owen and Sassoon in Edinburgh: behind the lines", *The Weekend Scotsman*, December 1st, 1973; Eastwood, Martin, "In remembrance of two poets", *The Weekend Scotsman*, 11 November, 1978; Sassoon Siegfried, "War diaries: haunted by the ghosts of the trenches", *The Sunday Telegraph*, March 6, 1983; Brogan, Colm, "From 'bitter safety' the Cry for Poetic Injustice", *The Glasgow Herald*, October 6, 1964; *The Buckle, May, 1968*, Edinburgh, Lindsay & Co., 1968

WILFRED OWEN *(p. 265)*
McAra, Charles, "Wilfred Owen's sojourn in the city", *Edinburgh Evening News*, December 30, 1950; Welland, Dennis, "Sassoon on Owen", *The Times Literary Supplement*, May 31, 1974; Coghill, Hamish, A Friendship born in the hell of war, *Evening News*, November 3, 1979; *Not about heroes: the friendship of Siegfried Sassoon and Wilfred Owen*, MacDonald, Stephen, (programme), Edinburgh Festival Fringe, 1982

DR HENRY LITTLEJOHN *(p. 268)*
"Fathers of the City, Vol. 3", *Extracts from Edinburgh Evening Express*, 1882-1883; C.T.S., "Obituary: Sir Henry Duncan Littlejohn, *M.D., LL.D., F.R.C.S.E.* ", *Edinburgh Medical Journal*, Vol. XIII, no. 5, Edinburgh, Oliver & Boyd, 1914; Tait, Haldane Philip, *A Doctor and Two Policemen*, Edinburgh, Edinburgh Corporation, 1974

BAILIE JAMES POLLARD *(p. 269)*
"Bailie Pollard", *Edinburgh Citizen and Portobello Advertiser, 1897*

ROBERT MORHAM *(p. 270)*
"Fathers of the City, Vol. 1", extracts from *Edinburgh Evening Express*, 1882-1883; Eddington, Alexander, *Edinburgh and*

the Lothians at the opening of the twentieth century, Brighton, Pike, 1904

PROFESSOR DAVID MASSON *(p. 273)*
Quasi Cursores: portraits of the high officers and professors of the University of Edinburgh at its tercentenary festival, Edinburgh, Constable 1884

ANDREW CARNEGIE *(p. 274)*
The Carnegie Dunfermline Trust, *Carnegie Year – 1985 commemorates Dunfermline boy who became the world's richest man – and its most famous philanthropist:* press release, 1984, typescript; Edinburgh City Libraries *Most potent agency: the building and development of Edinburgh Central Library*, by A. G. D. White, Edinburgh, Edinburgh City Libraries, 1984

MORNINGSIDE WRITERS AND ARTISTS *(p. 278)*
About St Matthew's, Morningside: the book of the bazaar, Edinburgh, R. & R. Clark, 1908; Cochrane, Robert, *Pentland walks, with their literary and historical associations*, Edinburgh, Andrew Elliot, 1918

WILLIAM MAIR *(p. 279)*
Mair, William, *A City View: a collection of press cuttings concerning William Mair from The Scotsman, The Evening Dispatch, Edinburgh Evening News, Journal of the American Pharmaceutical Association, The Chemist and Druggist, The Pharmaceutical Journal* and the *Wine Trade Review*, 1936-37; "William Mair: obituary", *The Scotsman*, December 2, 1948; Wedd, Deirdre, *(Letter to Charles J. Smith concerning William Mair, undated)*; Waugh, Joseph Laing, *Robbie Doo*, Dumfries, Thomas Hunter, Watson Co., 1912

ALEXANDER REID *(p. 281)*
(Collection of press cuttings on Alexander Reid from *Evening Dispatch*, 1958, *Edinburgh Evening News*, 1946-1982. *People's Journal*, 1969 and *The Scotsman*, 1958-1982); Reid, Alexander, *Two Scots Plays*, London, Collins, 1958

TOM MacDONALD *(p. 282)*
Morrison, David, ed., *Essays on Fionn MacColla*, Thurso, John Humphries, 1973; MacColla, Fionn, *Too long in this condition (Ro Fhada Mar So A Tha Mi)*, Thurso, John Humphries, 1975;

MacDiarmid, Hugh, "Scottish spirit incarnate", *Scots Independent*, September, 1975

GEORGE CAMPBELL HAY *(p. 284)*
Four Points of a saltire: the poetry of Sorley Maclean, George Campbell Hay, William Neill, Stuart MacGregor, Edinburgh, Reprographia, 1970; Smith, Iain Crichton, "The Heart of a nationalist poet", *Scotsman*, August 11, 1984; Meek, Donald, "Land and Loyalty", the Gaelic verse of George Campbell Hay, *Chapman* 39, Vol. 8, No. 2, Edinburgh, Autumn 1984; Rankin, Robert A., "George Campbell Hay as I knew him", *Chapman* 40, Vol. VIII, No. 3, Edinburgh, Spring 1985

DR STUART MacGREGOR *(p. 286)*
Collection of press cuttings on Stuart MacGregor, from *The Scotsman* and *Evening News and Dispatch*, 1967-1973; M.S.L., "S. W. MacGregor, M.B., Ch.B., D.P.H.", London, *British Medical Journal* February 24, 1973; "A Tribute to Dr Stuart William MacGregor, M.B., Ch.B., D.P.H.*" Community Health Aids Newsletter*, Vol. 2, No. 2, Kingston, University of the West Indies, March, 1973; MacGregor, Stuart, *The Myrtle and the ivy*, Edinburgh, M. Macdonald, 1967; MacGregor, Stuart, *The Sinner*, London, Calder & Boyars, 1973

LORD GUTHRIE *(p. 301)*
Orr, Robert Low, *Lord Guthrie: a memoir*, London, Hodder & Stoughton, 1923

ROBERT ALEXANDER *(p. 288)*
Caw, James L., *Scottish Painting Past and Present, 1620-1908*, Edinburgh, Jack, 1908

GOURLAY STEELL *(p. 288)*
As for Robert Alexander

GEORGE SINCLARE *(p. 290)*
Sinclare, George, *Satan's invisible world discovered*, Edinburgh, Thomas George Stevenson, 1831

BAILIE JAMES COLSTON *(p. 291)*
Colston, James, *The Edinburgh and district water supply: a historical sketch*, Edinburgh, privately printed, 1890; "Judge Colston", *Edinburgh Citizen and Portobello Advertiser*, 1897

THE SIX-FOOT-HIGH CLUB *(p. 294)*
Stevenson, Robert Louis, *St Ives*, London, Dent, 1897

THE STEVENSON FAMILY *(p. 297)*
Guthrie, Charles John, *Lord, Robert Louis Stevenson: some personal recollections*, Edinburgh, W. Green & Son, 1924; Kennedy, June, "R. L. Stevenson's Edinburgh", *Coming Events in Britain*, London, B.T.A., November, 1958

JOHN TODD *(p. 297)*
Stevenson, Robert Louis, *Memories and Portraits*, London, Chatto & Windus, 1887

AN OLD SCOTS GARDENER *(p. 298)*
As for John Todd above

This Bibliography should be used in conjunction with that provided in Volume 2

INDEX

316

324

328

329

HUNTERS TRYST

SWAN